PRACTICE

SPANISH

The Handbook

PRACTICE & IMPROVE YOUR

SPANISH

The Handbook

José Amodia Gómez
John Pride

PASSPORT BOOKS
a division of *NTC Publishing Group*
Lincolnwood, Illinois USA

Note
All the characters and incidents in this book and the
accompanying recorded material are fictitious and bear no
relation to any known person, firm or company.

José Amodia Gómez, the author of "Practice & Improve Your
Spanish", has been teaching Spanish for more than twenty
years. He has published a number of works on Spanish politics.
He is also the author of several English and Spanish courses.

John Pride, co-author of this Handbook, is an experienced
writer of language teaching material and has been responsible
for the publication of a number of language courses.

1994 Printing

This edition first published in 1988 by Passport Books, a division of
NTC Publishing Group, 4255 West Touhy Avenue,
Lincolnwood, Illinois 60646-1975 U.S.A.
Developed by Harrap Limited.
©Harrap Limited, 1986. All rights reserved.
No part of this book may be reproduced, stored in a retrieval
system, or transmitted in any form, or by any means,
electronic, mechanical, photocopying or otherwise, without the
prior permission of NTC Publishing Group.
Manufactured in the United States of America.

3 4 5 6 7 8 9 ML 9 8 7 6 5 4

CONTENTS

About the "Practice & Improve" series

Passport Books' "Practice & Improve" series represents a new kind of approach to learning languages. The idea is to mirror as closely as possible the experience of living in a foreign country and hearing the language spoken in natural, day-to-day conversations. The cassettes are designed for relaxed listening on a car stereo or a Walkman, so you can play them while you are traveling to work, going to school, doing housework and so on.

The story

Each course consists of a combination of drama and practice materials interspersed with music. The dramatic scenes build into a story − rather similar to a radio play. The recordings are all in stereo and include realistic sound effects which serve both to create the atmosphere and to give important clues about what is happening.

All recorded material is in the target language. The script has been carefully constructed to allow for the emphasis and repetition of important elements. Otherwise, however, the conversation that you will hear is completely authentic, and deliberately includes all the hesitations and interjections of normal speech.

The course is intended for entertaining and *repeated* listening. It is therefore not necessary for you to try and understand every word right away. The important thing, particularly if you have only a basic knowledge of your chosen language, is to be patient: don't become obsessed with details. Each time you listen you will understand more − words and phrases will become increasingly familiar and will start to stick in your mind.

The practices

The practice sections highlight particular language points that occur in the preceding or following scene of the story. They allow you to review the basic elements of structure and grammar while concentrating on the language you are likely to need when traveling or working abroad. You can join in with the practices if you want, or simply think the answers to yourself — it's up to you. Most sections have a gentle background music accompaniment; this is to promote a relaxed response and, at a more subliminal level, to aid your retention of the language.

Accent

The practices are spoken by actors whose native accent is, as far as possible, a neutral and agreed standard for the language being learned. They provide the models for your pronunciation.

Within the story, on the other hand, different regional accents are present in order to familiarize you with the varying pronunciations you are likely to encounter when traveling through different areas or countries.

The Guide

The story and the practices are explained and commented on by a "Guide", who provides the continuity between the different sections and effectively replaces the headings and instructions you find in conventional language courses.

The Guide and Handbook

The Guide provides an exact transcript of the words spoken on tape. If you have problems understanding a particular word or phrase, you can look it up in the Guide and then refer to the appropriate section in the Handbook or to a dictionary.

The Handbook is provided as a source of reference and instruction. It contains summaries of the scenes and practices as well as notes, appendices and wordlists. (The wordlists, by the way, are not intended to be exhaustive: they cover only the less common words in the language.)

Remember that these books are not intended to be studied in a formal way. They are to prime and prompt you for your main activity — listening.

Level

It is important to bear in mind that "Practice & Improve" is *not an introductory course*. It will not be suitable for you if you have no previous knowledge of the language you are studying. However, if you have a basic background—from learning in school or taking a beginner's course—you'll find the approach ideal, positively refreshing.

The two courses available are set up in order of difficulty. "Practice & Improve Your Spanish" gives more review of the basic points of grammar at an early stage. If you are a bit rusty on the basics, you'll find you need that course. However, if you are already confident of your grasp of the grammar and ground rules, you can go straight into "Practice & Improve Your Spanish PLUS," if you wish: there's no need to work through the first course.

The level you achieve will depend largely on your own aptitude and application. The courses offer you the chance to become fluent in your chosen language, given time and practice. If, on the other hand, you are studying for a particular purpose – an oral exam, a business trip or a vacation, for instance – you can make great progress simply by listening through and concentrating on the particular situations and areas of language that interest you. The courses are designed for complete flexibility: the end product of learning is ultimately dependent on your own requirements and motivation.

How to Study

A relaxed approach

The most important thing is to be relaxed. Part of the
philosophy underlying the course is based on the increased
learning efficiency achieved by *not* concentrating too hard on
the material you are studying. This is why "Practice & Improve" is ideal for listening to while you are engaged in some
other task.

First things first

Following these instructions there is a brief outline of the main
features of the target language – its similarities to and
differences from English. If your knowledge is very rusty, you
might like to read through this to refresh your memory. If you
have trouble with any of the descriptive terms used, there is
a short glossary at the back of the book to help you.

Using the course

The best approach is to read through the summaries of the
scenes and practices for the tape you are going to listen to.
These summaries are contained at the top of every other page
in this Handbook. It shouldn't take you long to look through
them–but don't try to do too much at once: one side of a cassette at a time will be sufficient.

Now you are ready to listen to the tape. Play one side all the
way through while the summaries are fresh in your mind.

Listen through again. This time you can join in with the practice sections if you wish and rewind the cassette selectively to listen to certain sections again. You can keep repeating this process as often as you like and, as you do so, you will find that you will become more and more at ease with the language you hear. You will soon begin to anticipate words and phrases, rather like picking up the lyrics of a song: this is excellent − it means that you are starting to *think* in the language.

As you listen through, you will also find that sections which appeared difficult to understand will gradually become clear to you as the context surrounding them becomes more familiar. You can, of course, aid this process by referring to the wordlists, notes and appendices in the Handbook. But (unless you are completely lost) don't do this at too early a stage: it's important not to become obsessed by details of grammar and meaning before you have given yourself a chance to "discover" the language. Your learning and retention will be much better if it comes as a result of absorbing the target language rather than as a response to a lot of rules and translations in your own language.

Take it easy!

The process described applies to each cassette, of course. Don't try to rush it: give each cassette side a "fair hearing" before going on to the next. However, you shouldn't take this to extremes. If you start to become bored with a cassette, you should immediately go on to the next one.

Enjoyment is important

These recommendations are designed to help you get the most out of "Practice & Improve your Spanish". Ultimately, of course, the way to study the materials is up to you. You may find it impossible to break the habit of a lifetime, and find yourself sitting down at a desk with the Listening Guide and Handbook as you listen to the cassettes. If you are happier this way, then that is the best approach to adopt. Above all, you should make sure you enjoy the activity of language learning.

Just bear in mind that much of the research into language learning indicates that a relaxed attitude pays off and that the idea of learning a language structure by structure is *not* the most effective strategy. The development of familiarity with a new language can be seen more as the process of an artist gradually filling in the details of a canvas than as an analogy with, let's say, bricklaying.

The Spanish Language

Similarities

Although English and Spanish are not members of the same family of languages, they share a number of features which will help the native speaker of English. The most obvious is that many words in both languages share the same root, coming mainly from Latin, from which Spanish is directly derived. There can be little doubt about the meaning of words like **civilización** *(civilization)*, **café** *(café* or *coffee)*, **aire** *(air);* others take a bit more recognizing: **puerto** *(port)*, **naranja** *(orange)*, **azul** *(blue)*. Many words, too, have come into English from Spanish such as **tomate** *(tomato)*, **patata** *(potato)*, while they both share various international 20th-century words like **teléfono** *(telephone)*, **televisión** *(television)*, **béisbol** *(baseball)*.

As a 'world' language Spanish, like English, has been open to many influences and so has a range of vocabulary which derives from many sources. It is the most widely spoken of all the Romance languages – a grouping which includes French, Italian and Portuguese – and, again like English, is spoken with a range of regional and national accents. Argentinian and Mexican Spanish are as distinct from Castilian Spanish (the accepted standard in Spain) as American and Australian English are from British English.

Differences

NOUNS AND ARTICLES

Spanish nouns are classified as either masculine or feminine, whether they refer to people, in which case the gender is obvious and logical, or things, where it is not obvious why they should be masculine or feminine. Fortunately there are some clues. The vast majority of nouns ending in **-o** are masculine and those in **-a** are feminine, although there are exceptions; words ending in **-ción** are also feminine. Forming the plural is easy. You just add **-s** if the noun ends in a vowel and **-es** if it ends in a consonant. The articles themselves also reflect gender and whether the noun is singular or plural.

ADJECTIVES

These also reflect both gender and number, 'agreeing' with the noun they describe. For the most part Spanish adjectives follow the noun, although there are a small number which precede it. A few adjectives differ in meaning according to whether they precede or follow a noun.

VERBS

These show far more inflections than their English counterparts. Indeed the verb ending is all-important in Spanish because it is frequently the only way of knowing not only the tense but also who the subject is. This is because, more often than not, the subject pronouns (**yo** *I,* **tú** *you,* etc.) are not used, being reserved usually for emphasis or for identification where absolutely necessary. However this is not as much of a problem as it sounds and is, in fact, quite an economical way of conveying meaning.

Like most languages, Spanish has its share of irregular verbs which one has to learn. An interesting feature of Spanish is that it has two verbs *to be* (**ser** and **estar**). These are not, unfortunately, interchangeable but one soon learns which one to use for what purpose. There are also two verbs *to have;* one (**tener**) is used to denote possession, the other (**haber**) to form compound tenses like the perfect.

The tenses are used in quite a similar way to the English ones, but there are a few differences, such as using the present to describe actions begun in the past which are still going on, where we would use the perfect – *I haven't seen him for years* **Hace años que no le veo.**

THE SUBJUNCTIVE

This is very important in Spanish, much more so than in English or French, and is widely used in everyday speech. It describes very often a mood of uncertainty or doubt, sometimes the hypothetical statement (e.g. *if I were* …); it also follows a variety of conjunctions and verbs expressing emotions and desires where people other than the speaker are involved. The Appendix will guide you on these points.

FORMS OF ADDRESS

In English the word *you* can refer to one or more than one person, male or female, and of any relationship to the speaker. Spanish has a highly developed sense of social proprieties and has four ways of expressing this simple concept: **tú** is used to address a relative, close friend or colleague of similar status to your own, a child, a social inferior or an animal; **vosotros** (feminine **vosotras**) covers more than one such person. For all other people – mere acquaintances, your social and business superiors – you use **usted** for one person and **ustedes** for more than one. It is always best to follow the lead of a native speaker in deciding which one to use – it is advisable to start with **usted** and **ustedes.**

PRONUNCIATION

An encouraging note to end on. Spanish pronunciation is straightforward and follows regular rules regarding individual letters and stress. The spelling also closely reflects the pronunciation and **h** is the only silent letter. This means that you can hear grammatical changes in speech, which helps you to learn the language all the more easily. There are a few points to look out for:
b and **v** normally sound the same (like a soft English *b*), although many speakers are inconsistent and often make them sound different.
c before **e** and **i**, and also **z** are pronounced like the *th* in *thin* in Castilian Spanish. However in some regions of Spain and all over Spanish America they are pronounced like *s*.
ch, **ll** and **ñ** are separate letters of the alphabet and are treated as such in dictionaries. **ch** is pronounced as in *church*, **ll** like *lli* in *million,* and **ñ** like *ni* in *onion.*
j, and **g** before **e** and **i**, are pronounced like the Scottish *ch* in *loch*.

THE PARIS AGENCY

Cassette 1   Side 1
A spring day

SCENE 1: Madrid – in Julio Gómez's car

The action begins in the morning. It is a lovely spring day
and Julio is giving a friend a lift to work. Their offices are in
the centre of Madrid. Julio leaves his car in the company's
parking lot and proceeds to his office where he greets
various colleagues. One of them, Antonio, wants an
advertisement translated into various languages and seeks
Julio's advice. Julio recommends an agency but cannot
remember their telephone number. He goes to his office to
find it because his own secretary is away.

LANGUAGE NOTES

 5 **¿Dónde te dejo?**   *Where shall I drop you?*
51 **¿Puedo pedírselo a Marisa?**   *Can I ask Marisa for it?*
    See Appendix Q for the position of object pronouns.
    Remember that **poder (ue)** is root changing (Appendix D).

15 **Mire, allí tiene un sitio**   *Look, there's a place over there*
35 **Mira, este anuncio**   *Look, this advertisement*
    Mire is the **usted** command form, **mira** the **tú** form
    (App. C).

35 **alemán e italiano**   *German and Italian*
    Note that **e** is used before words starting in **i** or **hi.**

44 **¿Conoces una buena?**   *Do you know a good one?*
    ¿Sabes su número de teléfono?   *Do you know its phone
    number?*
    Conocer *to know* (places, people), **saber** *to know* (facts).

2

WORDLIST

vamos a llegar tarde	we're going to be late
falta muy poco	there's not very far to go
la época	time of the year
la primavera	spring
¿dónde te dejo?	where shall I drop you?
trabajar	to work
el edificio	building
vale	o.k., fine
gracias por haberme traído	thanks for bringing me
no hay de qué	you're welcome
hasta otro día	good-bye for now
¿dónde aparco?	where can I park?
el conserje	custodian
allí tiene un sitio	there's a place over there
buenos de verdad	a fine day indeed
¿qué? ¿bien?	how are things? o.k.?
¿dispones de un momento?	have you got a moment?
ven a mi despacho	come to my office
te veo muy alegre	you look very happy
el anuncio	advertisement
no me parece muy difícil	it doesn't seem very difficult
tan fácil	so easy
bastante	quite
cualquier agencia de traducciones puede hacerlo	any translation agency can do it
solemos usar	we usually use
algo así como	something like
todos los idiomas	every language
¿te has quedado solo?	are you on your own?
no me importa	I don't mind
voy a buscarte	I'll go get you
a veces	sometimes
antes del ...	before the ...

PRACTICE 1: Greetings

The guide introduces you to the practice section, telling
you that this is a program in which you learn by listening.
He tells you to listen to the recordings several times and in
that way you'll understand a great deal of Spanish. He will
help you along and you'll start by listening again to the
various greetings you heard in Scene 1. When you have
listened a few times repeat what you have heard in the
pauses. Do this several times until you are satisfied.

LANGUAGE NOTES

1 **Es éste un programa en el que se aprende escuchando**
This is a program in which one learns by listening
It is very common in Spanish for the verb to come before
the subject, as here with **Es éste ...** If this were a question,
the tone of voice in speech and the inverted question mark
in writing would indicate it. Note that **programa** is a
masculine noun and so you have **el que** meaning *which*.

2 **Escuche las grabaciones**   *Listen to the recordings*
The guide talks to you politely and formally as **usted,** using
the appropriate verb forms **escuche** and **llegará** (Appendix
C, E) and the object pronoun **le** instead of **te** (Appendix Q).

3 **llegará a comprender**   *you'll get to learn*
4 **Yo le acompañaré**   *I'll accompany you*
For the future tense see Appendix E.

5 **Vamos a escuchar**   *Let's listen to*
Vamos a followed by the infinitive of the verb is the usual
way of suggesting that we do something: **vamos a ver** *let's
see*. On its own **vamos** can mean *let's go* or *we're going*
or *we go*.

WORDLIST

el saludo	greeting
el guía	guide
bienvenido	welcome
éste	this, this one (pronoun)
el programa	program
el que	which
se aprende	one learns
escuchando	by listening
escuche	listen to
la grabación	recording
una y otra vez	several times
de ese modo	in that way
llegará a comprender	you'll get to understand
le	you
acompañaré	I'll accompany
vamos a escuchar	let's listen to
de nuevo	again
la forma	form, way
saludar	to greet
la mujer	woman
el hombre	man
tú	you

PRACTICE 2: Seeking information

This section is about seeking information. Once again your guide takes you through a series of questions, answers and comments based on the language of Scene 1. Listen as often as you feel necessary and repeat in the pauses.

LANGUAGE NOTES

1 **alguien quiere saber algo**   *somebody wants to know something*
Two very useful little words here: **alguien** *somebody, someone* and **algo** *something, anything.*

3 **Tengo poco tiempo**   *I haven't got much time*
This says literally *I have little time* and is the usual Spanish way of making statements like this. You'll hear the guide make a sarcastic comment **¡Poco tiempo es!** when the lady tells the man it'll only take an instant.

4 **Sólo un instante**   *Only an instant*
Note **sólo** *only;* **solo** without an accent means *alone* as in **¿Te has quedado solo?** in Scene 1.

14 **lo tienes en tu oficina**   *You've got it in your office*
Note **tu** (with no accent) meaning *your* which is used in reference to people you address as **tú** (with an accent).

18 **¿Cómo?**   *What?*
¿Cómo? really means *how?* but is regularly used to indicate that you have not heard something or cannot believe it.

22 **el trabajo continúa**   *the work goes on*
Listen carefully and note how **continúa** is stressed on the **ú.**

WORDLIST

solicitar	to ask for, seek
la información	information
alguien	somebody, someone
querer (ie)	to want
algo	something
tengo poco tiempo	I haven't got much time
sólo	only
el instante	instant
aquí	here
recordar (ue)	to remember
claro	of course
la secretaria	secretary
¿cómo?	what?
hoy	today
tiene dos semanas de vacaciones	she has two weeks' holiday
pero	but
el trabajo	work
continuar	to go on, continue

SCENE 2: Madrid – in the offices of PATESA

The two characters in this scene are standing by the door to Julio Gómez's office. One of them, Luisa Ortega, is looking for Julio. The other, a workman, is apparently taking everything out of the office. Luisa, who does not know the place, requests information but the workman is unwilling or unable to provide it. All her questions about Julio himself, the number of his office, or why the furniture is being removed receive rather unhelpful answers. The workman, who does not seem to have a high opinion of office people, just wants to get on with his job. In the end Luisa seems to give up.

LANGUAGE NOTES

5   **Estoy buscando a don Julio Gómez**   *I'm looking for don Julio Gómez*
Note the personal **a** here which is used when the direct object of a verb is a person. Remember that **don** (feminine **doña**) is a courtesy title used with the first name.

21   **No hay nadie**   *There's nobody/There isn't anybody (there)*
Note the double negative in Spanish: *there isn't nobody.*

28   **Supongo que no**   *I suppose not*
There are numerous expressions in Spanish which use **que** in this manner: **supongo que sí** *I suppose so,* **creo que sí** *I think so,* **creo que no** *I don't think so.*

31   **A mí me dijeron que vaciase esta oficina**   *They told me to clear this office* (literally *that I should clear*)
A mí is often added for emphasis before **me** *to me.*

WORDLIST

¿qué hay?	what's up? what do you want?
pues no lo sé	well, I don't know
ésta	this, this one (pronoun)
doscientos quince	two hundred and fifteen
así es	that's right, it is
me parece que	I think that
la de	the one of, belonging to
pudiera ser	it could be
¿qué está haciendo?	what are you doing?
vaciar	to empty, clear
tengo que	I have to
sacar	to take out
todo	everything, all
cambiar de	to change, move
eso	that
dejar	to leave
le	him, for him, to him
el recado	message
ahí fuera	out there
nadie	nobody, no one
llegan tarde	they're late
como de costumbre	as usual
tendrá	will have
por lo tanto	therefore
supongo que no	I suppose not
entonces	then
¡yo que sé!	how do I know!
me dijeron que vaciase	they told me to clear
poner	to put
todas estas cosas	all these things
ahí	there
el pasillo	corridor
luego	then, after that

PRACTICE 3: The numbers

This gives you an opportunity to practise the numbers, a list of which you will find in the Appendix. A woman who is looking for don Julio's office and another man who works in the same building are talking about office numbers. Listen several times to what they have to say and then repeat in the pauses on the tape. Do this as often as you think necessary.

LANGUAGE NOTES

2 **Oigamos otra vez lo que dice**   *Let's hear again what she says*
Lo que means *what* but does not ask a question (you need **¿qué?** for that). **Lo que** is a link word which does not refer to a specific thing but rather to a whole idea, sentence, etc., with the sense of *that which*

7 **La doscientos quince**   *Two hundred and fifteen*
La is used with the number here as it refers to the number of the office which is **la oficina.**

9 **La mía es**   *Mine is*
The feminine form **la mía** is used because it refers to **mi oficina** which is feminine. If the speaker were referring to his/her car (**mi coche** is masculine) he/she would say **el mío.**

16 **Escuchemos ahora los números de forma más sistemática**
Now let's listen to the numbers in a more systematic way
Note the use of **de** with **forma.** You'll also find it used with **manera** *manner, way:* **de manera más sistemática.**

28 **Y a partir de cien ...**   *And from a hundred ...*
You'll often find **a partir de** meaning *from* in the sense of *starting from/with.*

WORDLIST

oír	to hear
oigamos	let's hear
lo que	what
decir	to say, tell
dice	she's saying
indicar	to point to
la mía	mine
escuchemos	let's listen to
sistemático	systematic
hasta	up to, as far as
o	or
a partir de	(starting) from
llegar	to arrive, come

SCENE 3: Madrid – in the offices of PATESA

Luisa has at last been able to locate Julio in the Patesa
building. He is in his secretary's office, still looking for the
translation agency's telephone number. You will remember
that his secretary was away on holiday. Confusion ensues
when Luisa and Julio meet. They don't know each other.
Julio thinks that Luisa has come to help him. You will
soon know why. And then, when the misunderstanding has
been cleared up, Julio wants to take Luisa to his office,
but doesn't know that his office ... Then the telephone
rings. It is Antonio. He wants to get in touch with the
translation agency and needs their number.

LANGUAGE NOTES

13 **Bromeaba**   *I was joking*
This is an imperfect form, as are **era** *you were* (19) and
estaban vaciándolo *they were emptying* (32). We also have
perfects in this scene, **he venido** *I've come* (27), **ha
venido** *has come* (15), **han hablado** *they have spoken* (24),
and a preterite **pensé** *I thought* (19). See Appendices F, G
and H.

33 **Dígame**   *Hello*   **Sí, al aparato**   *Yes, speaking*
Two standard expressions to use when answering the phone.

20 **¿En qué puedo servirla?**   *(How) can I help you?*
You'll hear this expression in shops, banks etc. If you are
talking to a male you would say **¿En qué puedo servirle?**

WORDLIST

¿dónde estará?	where can ... be?
el libro de direcciones	address book
suele ponerlo	usually puts it
por aquí	over here
acabar de	to have just
había	there was, there were
siempre	always
la	her; you (feminine)
¿de veras?	really?
bromeaba	I was joking
ha venido	has come
sustituir	to replace
perdone	I'm sorry, excuse me
me llamo	my name is
lo siento	I'm sorry
pensé	I thought
era	you were
¿en qué puedo servirla?	(how) can I help you?
¿no le dice nada mi nombre?	doesn't my name mean anything to you?
no me suena	it doesn't ring a bell
¿no le han hablado?	haven't they spoken to you?
el proyecto	project, plan
oí	I heard
a eso he venido	that's what I've come for
venga	come (**usted** command form)
ya no	no longer
¿cómo dice?	what do you mean?
dígame	hello
sí, al aparato	speaking

PRACTICE 4: Listen in order to understand (1)

Two people are talking about how one learns a language by listening to it and how important it is try to catch the gist of what someone is saying even if you cannot understand every word. At the end the guide brings us back to the story where Julio was speaking on the phone.

LANGUAGE NOTES

2 **Hay que pedirles que repitan lo dicho**   *You must ask them to repeat what they said*
Hay que followed by an infinitive is often used to issue an instruction. Note the subjunctive after **pedir** (Appendix M).

4 **No le entiendo**   *I don't understand you*
Entender is another example of a root changing verb. We've already come across various forms of **poder, recordar, querer** and some others. See Appendix D for full treatment.

4 **Habla usted muy de prisa**   *You speak very quickly*
Here's another example of the verb coming before the subject. Also **se requiere práctica** *practice is required* (7).

11 **¿Cuántas horas tuvo que pasar practicando?**   *How many hours did you have to spend practising?*
Tuvo is part of the preterite tense of **tener** (Appendix H).

19 **Ahora haga algo parecido con el español**   *Now do something similar with Spanish*
These speakers are on **usted** terms. Note the **usted** imperatives like **haga: pase** *spend* (19), **siga** *go on* (24), **acostúmbrese** *get used to* (25), **olvídese** *forget* (27), **trate** *try* (27), **escuche** *listen* (31), **practique** *practise* (34).

WORDLIST

de prisa	quickly
al menos	at least
así parece	so it seems
hay que	one must
repetir (i)	to repeat
lo dicho	what was said
entender (ie)	to understand
la velocidad	speed
lo parece	it seems so
requerir (ie)	to require
propio	own
desde luego	of course
¿cuántas?	how many?
tuvo que	you had to
pasar	to spend (of time)
practicar	to practise
haga algo parecido	do something similar
me haré viejo	I'll grow old
tanto	so much
al principio	at first
pocas palabras	few words
algunas no va ni a oírlas	some you won't even hear
no se preocupe	don't worry
siga escuchando	go on listening
acostúmbrese a	get used to
de acuerdo	all right, agreed
olvídese de	forget
trate de captar	try to grasp
el sentido general	gist, general sense
el tema	subject matter
poco a poco	little by little
esperemos que sí	let's hope so
practique	practise

SCENE 4: Madrid – in the offices of PATESA

Having provided Antonio with the necessary information Julio turns his attention back to Luisa, only to discover that she was right. His office is empty. Julio finds it hard to believe what has happened. His main concern seems to be rather trivial. But then he is so fond of coffee. Luisa, who saw the workman take the things out, suggests he take a look outside, in the corridor. Julio goes through the various items in the corridor but cannot find his beloved machine. Luisa finds it difficult to keep a straight face, but when Julio wants to go and find somebody to complain to she has to remind him that they are supposed to be having a meeting. Julio, very apologetic, postpones the meeting till the afternoon.

LANGUAGE NOTES

20 **Tal vez esté ahí fuera**   *Perhaps it's out there*
21 **Más vale que esté**   *It had better be*
Note the subjunctives (**esté**) here. See Appendix (M).

26 **No veo cafetera alguna**   *I can't see any coffee maker at all*
Alguno has a negative sense when it follows a noun.

45 **¿Cuánto tiempo ...?**   *How long ...?* (Lit. *How much time?*)

53 **¿a qué hora?**   *(at) what time?*
Remember; **tiempo** *time, weather;* **hora** *hour, time* (by clock).

55 **Hasta más tarde**   *See you later*
Note also: **hasta otro día** *goodbye for now,* **hasta mañana** *see you tomorrow,* **hasta el lunes** *see you on Monday* etc.

WORDLIST

llamar	to call
tiene que perdonar	you must excuse me
no tiene importancia	it doesn't matter
es que	the fact is
ya no lo es	no longer exists
lo que le estaba diciendo	what I was telling you
vacío	empty
ver	to see
¿qué ha pasado?	what's happened?
el lugar	place
sin decir ni una palabra	without saying a word
se fue	he went off
la cafetera	coffee making machine
la empresa	the company
tal vez	perhaps
más vale que esté	it had better be
armar un gran lío	to make a big fuss
ahí debajo	under there
el encargado de las oficinas	the office manager
hace unos diez minutos	about ten minutes ago
vaya	come on
no es para reírse	it's nothing to laugh about
tener gracia	to be funny
un poco	a little while
la verdad	the truth
quedar de acuerdo	to agree
dentro de una hora	in an hour
volver (ue)	to come back
¿le viene bien?	is that all right with you?
si le parece	if you like
aclarar	to clear up
¿a eso de las cuatro?	at about four?
hasta más tarde	see you later

PRACTICE 5: Where is?

This deals with where things are. Two people are reorganizing an office. The guide tells you what happens and then you hear the people talking about it as they get on with the reorganization. Look out for prepositions referring to place and remember **estar,** not **ser,** is used for location. Repeat in the pauses as usual.

LANGUAGE NOTES

2 **no encuentra la cafetera tampoco**   *he can't find the coffee maker either*
Here is another of the double negatives. **Tampoco** means *neither* and is used either after a verb with **no** preceding it (as here) or before a verb without **no.**

3 **¿Dónde estará?**   *Where can it be?*
Note how Spanish uses the future tense here.

6 **Esta oficina hay que arreglarla**   *This office needs to be organized*
This is another example of the use of **hay que** plus an infinitive to indicate that something has to be done.

11 **¿Qué vas a cambiar la oficina?**   *Are you going to change the office?*
Cambiar la oficina means that changes are going to be made in the office; **cambiar de oficinas** means *to change offices.*

31 **Pues está dentro de este cajón**   *Well it's in this big box*
The ending **ón** usually indicates size. Hence **el cajón** means *big box, chest, crate.* It comes from **la caja** *box.* Similarly **la silla** *chair* gives us **el sillón** *armchair.*

WORDLIST

se ha quedado	he's been left
no ... tampoco	not ... either
tampoco	neither
arreglar	to arrange, organize
al lado de	next to, at the side of
el cuadro	picture
la pared	wall
el sillón	armchair
la máquina de escribir	typewriter
encima de	on top of
la mesita	small table
de modo distinto	in a different way
mover (ue)	to move
debajo de	under
va a quedar muy bien	it's going to be fine
por lo menos	at least
mejor ordenada	better organized
la cartera	briefcase; wallet
¿dónde la dejaste?	where did you leave it?
estar seguro	to be sure
dentro de	in, inside
el cajón	big box, crate
aquel mismo día	that same day
por la tarde	in the afternoon

SCENE 5: Madrid – in the offices of PATESA

At the beginning of this scene Luisa is talking to the managing director of PATESA. We join the conversation towards the end. The director is impressed by the fact that Luisa has been put in charge of the Paris project. Luisa has to decline the invitation to have coffee because it is time to go and see Julio. The scene moves now to Julio's empty office. After the initial greetings and apologies, Julio admits that his memory is not very good. He never remembers names. The situation is clarified and our two characters are about to start their discussion when the unfriendly workman comes in to bring new furniture into the office. It looks as if Luisa's meeting with Julio is doomed not to take place.

LANGUAGE NOTES

11 **¿Quiere tomar un café?**   *Would you like coffee?*
Remember **tomar** is used for *to have* with food and drink.

21 **Adelante**   *Come in*
23 **Pase**   *Come in*
Both of these are in common use. To a person you address as **tú,** you would use **pasa** instead of **pase.**

37 **No te importará que te tutee ...**   *You won't mind if I call you tú ...*
Now that Julio and Luisa are established as colleagues they switch from **usted** to **tú.** It's advisable to let a native speaker make the decision but if you want to do it yourself this is the phrase to use.

WORDLIST

la ayuda	help
para eso estamos	that's what we're here for
estar contenta	to be pleased
así por las buenas	just like that
me hace mucha ilusión	I'm very thrilled about it
el trabajo	job
la edad	age
que me gusta	which I like
el ingeniero	engineer
le causará buena impresión	you'll be impressed by him
quedamos en vernos	we agreed to see each other
es casi la hora	it's almost time
si en algo pueda servirla	if I can help you in any way
adelante	come in
pase	come in
libre	free
siento lo de esta mañana	I'm sorry about this morning
tuve que dejarla plantada	I had to leave you abruptly
dígame	tell me
¿cómo dijo que se llamaba?	what did you say your name was?
se me olvidan los nombres	I forget names
la cara	face
casi nunca	almost never
no te importará que te tutee	you won't mind if I call you **tú**
preferir (ie)	to prefer
estar ocupado	to be busy
ya pasa de las cuatro	it's already past four
oiga	listen
yo me voy	I leave
meter	to put
empezar (ie)	to start, begin
probar (ue)	to try
no tengo ni idea	I haven't a clue

PRACTICE 6: How to apologize and introduce oneself

This section gives you the chance to listen and practise useful expressions for apologizing and for getting to know someone. Listen as often as you need to and repeat in the pauses.

LANGUAGE NOTES

1 **están empezando a conocerse**   *are beginning to get to know each other*
Conocerse *to get to know each other* is of course a reflexive verb. As you know reflexive verbs often have the meaning of *self,* e.g. **matarse** *to kill oneself.* However Spanish reflexive verbs do not always have this meaning as we've already seen with **irse** *to leave, go away.* See Appendix K.

18 **siento llegar tarde**   *I'm sorry I'm late*
To apologize for doing or not doing something all you have to do is add the appropriate infinitive to **siento: siento no haberlo hecho** *I'm sorry I haven't done it.*

20 **le dije a las cuatro**   *I told you four o'clock*
Dije is part of the preterite tense of **decir** and is, as you can see, irregular. You've already come across another form in **¿cómo dijo que se llamaba?** *what did you say your name was?* As there will be a good number of preterites in the next few sections this might be a good time to turn to Appendix H and brush up your knowledge of them.

25 **No te importará que te tutee ...**
You'll no doubt remember this expression from the previous scene. Note that **tutear** is used in the subjunctive as it comes after **importar que** (Appendix M).

WORDLIST

pedir (i) perdón	to apologize
darse a conocer	to introduce oneself
conocerse	to get to know each other
aunque	although
la dificultad	difficulty
la taza	cup
la culpa es mía	it's my fault
ha caído	it's fallen
el papel	paper
la ropa	clothes
a mí también	so do I, me too
por todas partes	everywhere
ya	already

PRACTICE 7: Types of company

We move here from social language to some useful business terminology. Our two speakers discuss who owns what. Pay particular attention to this practice section as it will help you enormously when you come to Scene 6. As usual listen as often you like and repeat in the pauses.

LANGUAGE NOTES

1 **se emplean algunas expresiones** *some expressions are used*

As you can see **se emplean** is a reflexive. Reflexive verbs are often used in Spanish when in English we would use a passive (the verb *to be* and a past participle) and here we have a typical example. Note some other useful examples: **se habla inglés** *English is spoken*, **se cambia dinero** *money changed*, **aquí se vende vino** *wine is sold here*.

4 **Dime algo** *Tell me something*

Dime is the form to use to someone you address as **tú.** We've already used the **usted** form **dígame.**

14 **otra en Brasil** *another one in Brazil*

Remember that **otro** means *another* as well as *other* and that you do not normally use **un** or **una** with it. Note the spelling of **Brasil.**

16 **¿Y la nuestra es la francesa?** *And ours is the French one?*

La nuestra stands for **nuestra empresa filial** and that explains why the feminine form is used. Remember that in expressions like **la francesa** Spanish does not use a word for *one,* as you saw in **la compañía matriz es la que encabeza un grupo de empresas** *the parent company is the one that heads a group of companies* (8).

WORDLIST

siguiente	following
emplearse	to be used
la expresión	expression
el mundo	world
los negocios	business
primero	first
dime	tell me
la compañía	company
formar parte	to be a part
el grupo	group
la empresa matriz	parent company
es decir	that is to say
encabezar	to head
la empresa filial	subsidiary company
además de	besides, apart from
la sucursal	branch (office)
controlar	to control
charlar	to chat
un rato	a while

SCENE 6: Madrid – in the offices of PATESA

Julio and Luisa are still looking for an empty office.
Eventually they find a room where they can sit and talk.
Or so they think. They start talking about their respective
firms and the connections between them. Julio does not
appear to know these connections very well. Luisa tries to
explain them, and mentions the Paris project too, but they
are interrupted once again. One of the secretaries is
leaving and wants to lock the office they are in. Julio
knows even less about the new project in Paris, even
though it affects him personally. He finds it hard to
believe what Luisa is telling him. To Paris and so soon? At
the insistence of the secretary, who is now getting rather
impatient, they both have to leave the office.

LANGUAGE NOTES

1 **Tiene que haber**   *There must be*
   Haber is the verb from which we have **hay** *there is/are,*
   había *there was/were,* **habrá** *there will be,* **habría**
   there would be, **ha habido** *there's been* and **había habido**
   there had been.

25 **Trabajaba**   *I used to work*
   This is one of a number of imperfect tense forms in this
   scene. Why not look at Appendix F and brush up on them?

41 **tengo que cerrar esta oficina antes de irme**   *I have to
   lock this office before I leave*

43 **deberíamos irnos**   *we ought to leave*
   These two sentences show how the reflexive pronoun
   changes according to the subject when the infinitive is used.

WORDLIST

tiene que haber	there must be
ésta de aquí	this one here
desocupado	unoccupied
pertenecer	to belong
al revés	the other way round
tenía entendido	I was under the impression
explicar	to explain
el cuarto	room
disponible	available
¡cómo que no!	why not?
cerrar (ie)	to close, lock
la puerta	door
la llave	key
¡por el amor de Dios!	for heaven's sake!
deberíamos	we ought, should
no era más qué	it was only
la curiosidad	curiosity
afectar	to affect
aceptar	to accept
¿el qué?	the what?
¿no recuerdas haberlo solicitado?	don't you remember requesting it/having requested it?
se me pasó por la cabeza	it did enter my head
interesarse	to be interested
no recuerdo que se decidiese nada	I don't remember anything being decided
o sea	that is to say
en avión	by air
el domingo que viene	next Sunday
si me hacen el favor	if you wouldn't mind
el fin de semana	weekend

Cassette 1   Side 2
The journey to Paris

SCENE 1: Madrid – in the car and in Julio's flat

Julio and Luisa are arriving by car at the former's flat. They go in and after the preliminary exchanges about having a drink and about the flat, they talk of their forthcoming trip to Paris. Julio has a telephone answering machine and switches it on to find out whether anybody has phoned him. Yes, there has been a call. From Marisa, his secretary. She is one of the most interesting characters in the story. Her recorded voice is going to tell Julio why he has to go to Paris and why his office was taken over by somebody else. You will also discover something about the relationship between Julio and his secretary. At the end of the scene Julio, embarrassed by the situation, wants to invite Luisa out to dinner, but Luisa declines.

LANGUAGE NOTES

12 **nos vemos el domingo por la noche o el lunes por la mañana**
We'll see each other Sunday night or Monday morning
Note how **por** is used to express periods of the day.

39 **No sé nada de ella**   *I don't know anything about her*
Here's another double negative: *I don't know nothing.*

58 **Te invito**   *I'm inviting you*
All you need say to invite someone out or for a drink, etc.

WORDLIST

el viaje	journey, trip
el piso	flat, apartment
enseguida	at once, straightaway
repentino	sudden
averiguar	to find out, check
el contestador automático	answering machine
útil	useful
fuera	out
con frecuencia	frequently
anoche	last night
proyectado	projected, planned
te vendrá bien	it'll suit you
a buenas horas	in good time
podrás pasarlo muy bien	you'll enjoy yourself
reunirme contigo	to join you, meet up with you
atrevido	bold, daring
trabajar a las órdenes de	to work under
si es guapa no te pases	if she's pretty don't go
vaya, vaya	well, I'll be darned
celoso	jealous
vendrán	they'll be coming
tendrás que buscarte	you'll have to find yourself
puesto que	as, since
en busca de	in search of
te estoy echando de menos	I miss you
pórtate bien	behave yourself
enviaré una tarjeta postal	I'll send a postcard
ni yo tampoco	neither do I, me neither
cenar	to have dinner
no hace falta	there's no need
a lo mejor	maybe, with luck
volver (ue) a llamar	to call again
otra vez	again

PRACTICE 1: A recorded message

Here you will hear two people discussing a telephone
answering machine and then you will listen to a message
that has been left on it. Finally the two speakers talk about
the message. Listen as often as you think fit and speak in
the pauses as usual.

LANGUAGE NOTES

12 **oye, mi coche está averiado**   *listen, my car's broken down*
Oye (tú) and **oiga (usted)** are good words to use to attract
someone's attention, especially on the phone.
Note that **estar** is used with **averiado**. This is because it is
a past participle describing a state, not an action. **Estar** is
always used in these circumstances.

13 **No sé por qué no funciona**   *I don't know why it isn't
working*
Funcionar and not **trabajar** is used about machinery.

15 **mañana por la mañana**   *tomorrow morning*
Here's another example of **por** being used to refer to a part
of the day; **ayer por la tarde** *yesterday afternoon*.

36 **Quiere que la lleve Armando**   *She wants Armando to
take her*
Because Elena wants someone else (i.e. Armando) to do
something the second verb **(lleve)** is a subjunctive preceded
by **que.** Literally it says *She wants that Armando take her.*
Note how it differs from **Armando quiere llevarla** *Armando
wants to take her* (See Appendix M.)

38 **Armando tendrá que llamarla por teléfono**
Armando will have to phone her
Tendrá is part of the future tense of **tener** (App. E).

WORDLIST

el mensaje	message
grabado	recorded
por qué	why
en cuanto a	as for, as regards
la máquina	machine
grabar	to record
la llamada telefónica	phone call
mecánico	mechanical
oye	listen
averiado	broken down
el garaje	garage
funcionar	to work
reparar	to repair
llevar	to take
mañana por la mañana	tomorrow morning
esta noche	tonight
la cuestión	question, matter

SCENE 2: Madrid – in the offices of PATESA

Julio is talking to Esteban, the man in charge of his department. He has gone to say goodbye before leaving for Paris. Esteban does not sound very happy. Julio's unexpected departure is going to create problems. Julio tries to appease him, and then broaches the question of his coffee-making machine. You will remember that Julio was upset by its disappearance when his office was emptied. Well, his boss feels that, in view of the serious problems he is going to face with Julio leaving so suddenly, it is rather frivolous to raise the question of a missing coffee machine. The departure is not very amicable!

LANGUAGE NOTES

13 **Podrías habernos avisado**   *You could have informed us*
Notice how to express *could have* in Spanish: the conditional of **poder** + the infinitive **haber** + the past participle, e.g. **podrían habérmelo dicho** *they could have told me about it.*

34 **no la encuentro por ninguna parte**   *I can't find it anywhere*
Another double negative: literally *I can't find it nowhere.*

38 **No esperarás que me preocupe**   *You can't expect me to worry,* **tú me pides que te busque**   *you ask me to look for*
Note the subjunctive after **esperar** and **pedir** (Appendix M).

46 **... que te vaya bien**   *I hope it goes well for you*
This literally says *may it go well for you,* **vaya** being a subjunctive form of **ir.** Esteban could have said **espero que te vaya bien** *I hope it goes well for you* (App. L, M).

WORDLIST

¿puedo pasar?	may I come in?
muy de golpe	very sudden
¿ya lo sabías?	you already knew?
a finales de	at the end of
me han dicho	they've told me
el avión	plane
avisar	to inform
antes	before, earlier
me temo que sí	I'm afraid so
arreglarse	to get organized
más bien	rather
tranquilo	quiet
menos mal	just as well
os	you, for you
crear	to create
desaparecer	to disappear
debió de pensar	must have thought
por ninguna parte	nowhere
eléctrico	electric
de color crema	cream coloured
comprar	to buy
el mes pasado	last month
esperar	to expect
preocuparse por	to worry about
el cliente	client, customer
que te vaya bien	I hope it goes well for you
si me lo permites	if you don't mind
seguir (i)	to carry on
faltaría más	of course
¡jo, qué mal humor!	phew, what a bad temper!

PRACTICE 2: The days of the week

Here you get the chance to practise the days of the week, not just repeating but answering questions about them. As usual listen several times and repeat in the pauses.

LANGUAGE NOTES

2 **El domingo que viene**   *Next Sunday*
Remember that the days are not capitalized and are masculine. Note too that if you want to say *on* a particular day **el** (or **los**) is sufficient, e.g. **me voy el lunes** *I'm leaving on Monday,* **va a Madrid los sábados** *he goes to Madrid on Saturdays.*

3 **Pregúntale cuándo es**   *Ask him when it is*
Preguntar means *to ask* in the sense of asking a question and so differs from **pedir** which means *to ask for* or to ask someone to do something as you've already seen.

5 **Empieza el lunes**   *It begins on Monday*
As you see **empezar** is a root changing verb. This might be *a good time to review your knowledge of these verbs by* turning to Appendix D.

20 **¿Y dentro de tres días?**   *And in three days' time?*
Dentro de is used for *in* regarding periods of time.

28 **Veamos si ya ha llegado**   *Let's see if she's already arrived*
Remember that the perfect tense in Spanish is formed with **haber** and the past participle (Appendix G).

WORDLIST

el domingo	Sunday
el lunes	Monday
el martes	Tuesday
el miércoles	Wednesday
el jueves	Thursday
el viernes	Friday
el sábado	Saturday
preguntar	to ask
cuántos días faltan	how many days are left
pasado mañana	the day after tomorrow
mientras tanto	meanwhile
veamos	let's see
la capital	capital

SCENE 3: At the airport and in Marta Vargas' car

Luisa arrives in Paris. Marta Vargas, an Argentinian girl who works for the same firm, has gone to meet her at the airport. Most of the scene takes place in Marta's car while travelling from the airport back to Paris. Marta tells Luisa about herself and her English husband, who is unemployed. They talk of various other things: nationalities, foreign languages, etc. Luisa has to find accommodations in Paris. Not an easy task it appears. But they refer to somebody who might be able to help. At the end of the scene Marta leaves Luisa at the door of the hotel where she is initially going to stay.

LANGUAGE NOTES

5 **¿Qué tal el vuelo?** *How was the flight?*
¿Qué tal? is a very useful question. It can be used in a friendly fashion to ask how someone is and also, with a noun as here, to ask how things are or were: **¿qué tal el hotel?** *how's the hotel?*

8 **Le agradezco mucho que haya venido a buscarme**
I'm grateful to you for having come to meet me
A very useful sentence. Note the subjunctive **haya venido.**

11 **hace años que vivo aquí** *I've lived here for years*
34 **llevo aquí varios años** *I've been here several years*
The present tense **vivo** and **llevo** is used because the action which was begun in the past is not yet over.

WORDLIST

buscar	to meet
encantado/a	pleased to meet you
¿qué tal el vuelo?	how was the flight?
cómodo	comfortable
agradecer	to thank
mismo	itself
las afueras	outskirts
casado (con)	married (to)
el marido	husband
dedicarse a la enseñanza	to be in teaching
estar en paro	to be unemployed
conseguir (i)	to get
siendo	being
el extranjero	foreigner
dominar el francés	to be fluent in French
lo cual	which
querer (ie) decir	to mean
el colegio	school, academy
el empleo	work, job
de momento	for the moment
ganar el pan	to be the breadwinner
adquirir (ie)	to acquire
la ventaja	advantage
regular	not too badly
defenderse (ie)	to manage, to get by
estudiar	to study
la habitación	room
prometer	to promise
ayudar	to help
el equipaje	luggage
traer	to bring, carry
bastar	to be enough

PRACTICE 3: Nationalities and occupations

This section gives you the chance to get a handle on some names of countries, nationalities and occupations. Follow your normal listening and repeating procedure.

LANGUAGE NOTES

2 **Es inglés** *He's English*
Remember that adjectives of nationality are not capitalized. Note that in the wordlist we have given you both the masculine and feminine forms.

13 **Es del Perú** *She's from Peru*
The names of most countries are feminine – **España, Inglaterra. El Perú** is masculine and is used with the definite article **el.**

15 **Mientras que el señor Gómez es de España** *While Sr. Gómez is from Spain*
Mientras que means *while* in the sense of *whereas,* but **mientras,** without **que** means *while* with the sense of during a period of time: **mientras estaba en Madrid fue al Prado** *while he was in Madrid he went to the Prado.*

32 **trabajo de profesor** *a job as a teacher*
It is usual to omit the indefinite article **(un, una)** with occupations unless you describe them in some way.

WORDLIST

la nacionalidad	nationality
atentamente	carefully
Inglaterra	England
inglés/inglesa	English
Francia	France
francés/francesa	French
vivir	to live
Alemania	Germany
alemán/alemana	German
Italia	Italy
italiano/italiana	Italian
el Perú	Peru
mientras que	while
España	Spain
español/española	Spanish
¿en qué trabaja?	what's his job?
el hombre de negocios	businessman
se habló	they spoke
el profesor de historia	history teacher
despacio	slowly
por partes	in sections
el oficinista	office worker
al día siguiente	next day
lo que pasa	what happens

SCENE 4: Paris – in the central offices of the holding company

Luisa goes to see Antoine Leconte at the holding company's central office in Paris. It is he who offered to help her find accommodations. By the way they talk to each other you will soon realize they have been quite good friends. After the initial greetings, a few polite questions about the trip and the hotel, and a little bit of nostalgia, the conversation moves on to more important matters. There is no room for Luisa and her team in the central offices of the company. M. Leconte has already arranged an appointment for Luisa with a realtor. It is time to go there, but M. Leconte tries to prolong her stay with an offer of coffee and an invitation to dinner. He seems to be showing more than a professional interest.

LANGUAGE NOTES

17 **Con su permiso**   *Excuse me*
This is a very useful polite phrase to have at your disposal. **Con permiso** is commonly used when you want to get through a crowd in a bus, shop, etc.

22 **No vais a ser más que cuatro o cinco. Y debería ser posible encontraros sitio**   *You won't be more than four or five. And it should be possible to find you room*
Leconte uses **vosotros** to refer to Luisa and her colleagues.

27 **tal vez sea mejor que no estemos aquí**   *perhaps it's best that we're not here*
32 **es mejor que tú hables**   *it's best for you to talk*
Note the subjunctives here (**sea, estemos, hables**).

WORDLIST

con su permiso	excuse me
¡qué sorpresa!	what a surprise!
agradable	pleasant
andar	to go
la queja	complaint
sentir (ie)	to feel
el terreno	ground
eso ya me lo suponía	that's what I imagined
tener sentido	to make sense
la organización	organization
distinto	different
de todos modos	anyway
la agencia inmobiliaria	realtor's office
sobre	about
juntos	together
no cambias nada	you don't change at all

PRACTICE 4: The time

Being able to cope with the time in a foreign language is obviously very important and here you have plenty of chance to practise telling the time in Spanish. There are questions and details about appointments and travelling. As usual listen several times and then repeat in the pauses.

LANGUAGE NOTES

1 **¿a qué hora?**   *(at) what time?*
5 **¿qué hora es?**   *what time is it?/what's the time?*
Make sure you learn these two essential questions.

4 **A las nueve y media**   *At half past nine*
16 **a la una y media**   *at half past one*
Remember that you must always use **las** with the hour except for **la una.**

14 **A las doce menos cuarto**   *At a quarter to twelve*
17 **a las cuatro y veinte**   *at twenty past four*
You use **y** to introduce time *past* the hour and **menos** time *to* the hour. Note that you do not use **un** with **cuarto.**

25 **¿a qué hora sale?**   *what time does it leave?*
Remember that **salir** has an irregular **yo** form – **salgo** and that it also has an irregular future tense – **saldré** etc.

WORDLIST

¿a qué hora?	(at) what time?
a las nueve y media	at half past nine
¿qué hora es?	what time is it?
son las nueve y media	it's half past nine
media hora	half an hour
después	after
el abogado	lawyer
a las doce menos cuarto	at a quarter to twelve
comer	to eat, have lunch
a las cuatro y veinte	at twenty past four
coger	to catch
el tren	train
salir	to leave, depart
el horario	schedule
las dieciséis veinte	16:20
las diecinueve cuarenta y cinco	19:45
es hora de	it's time to
volver (ue)	to return
hacer los preparativos	to prepare
la agencia de viajes	travel agency

SCENE 5: Madrid – at a travel agency

The scene flashes back to Madrid where Julio is in a travel agency making arrangements to go to Paris. He wants to book a flight. The conversation follows the normal pattern in such a situation. They talk about the choice of airlines, flight times, dates, reservations, etc. The scene concludes with some references to the various forms of payment.

LANGUAGE NOTES

6   **Cualquiera**   *Any one*
   Cualquiera here is a pronoun standing for **cualquier compañía** *any company*. You will have noticed that when **cualquiera** is used as an adjective with a noun the final **a** is dropped. The plural form is **cualesquier(a).**

24   **¿Vuelo de vuelta también?**   *Return flight as well?*
   It's useful to know certain terms relating to tickets and trips when traveling: **billete de ida y vuelta** *round-trip ticket,* **viaje de ida** *the trip out.*

31   **¿Cómo va a pagar el billete?**   *How are you going to pay for the ticket?*
   Try to remember that you do not use any equivalent for *for* when you use **pagar.** You've already come across other verbs like this in **buscar** *to look for* and **pedir** *to ask for.*

31   **¿En efectivo, con tarjeta de crédito, con cheque …?**
   In cash, by credit card, by cheque …?
   Note that you use **con** with **tarjeta de crédito** and **cheque.**

WORDLIST

el agente	agent
cualquiera	any one
la clase	class
turista	tourist
hacer la reserva	to make the reservation
el vuelo de vuelta	return flight
la ida	the trip out
reservar	to reserve
la plaza	place, seat
el día diez	tenth
pagar	to pay (for)
el billete	ticket
el efectivo	cash
la tarjeta de crédito	credit card
el cheque	cheque
veintidós mil	twenty two thousand
quinientos	five hundred
tenga	there you are
firmar	to sign
el resguardo	receipt

PRACTICE 5: Buying a plane ticket

There is some very useful language concerning buying an air ticket for you to practise here. Some new words and expressions are added to those you encountered in the last scene. Listen several times and then repeat in the pauses.

LANGUAGE NOTES

1 **acaba de sacar un billete**   *has just bought a ticket*
You've already seen **sacar** meaning *to take out, remove*. It is also used to refer to buying tickets of all kinds.

10 **¿Para cuándo lo quiere?**   *When do you want it for?*
Para el viernes   *For Friday*
Note that **para** is used to refer to future time.

12 **a las diez de la mañana**   *at 10 a.m.*
22 **a las cuatro de la tarde**   *at 4 p.m.*
De la mañana and **de la tarde** are used with time by the clock while **por la mañana** and **por la tarde** refer to the general period of the day.

13 **¿Hay algún vuelo por la tarde?**   *Is there any flight in the afternoon?*
Alguno drops the **o** before a masculine noun, like **bueno**.

15 **¿Cuánto tarda en llegar a Londres?**   *How long does it take to get to London?*
The usual way to express how long it takes to do something is to use **tardar en** followed by an infinitive. Note too **llegar** is followed by **a** when the destination is mentioned: **llegué a París a las dos** *I arrived in Paris at two.*

WORDLIST

sacar	to buy (tickets)
la serie	series
cuyo	whose
el uso	use
el billete de ida	one-way ticket
de ida y vuelta	round-trip
¿para cuándo lo quiere?	when do you want it for?
de la mañana	a.m., in the morning
algún	any
¿cuánto tarda en?	how long does it take to?
tardar en	to take (of time)
llegar a	to arrive in
hora inglesa	British time
de la tarde	p.m., in the afternoon
no lo ponga fecha	don't put a date on it
abierto	open
vuelva a escucharlo	listen to it again
suficiente	sufficient, enough
como quiera	as you like
el pasajero	passenger

SCENE 6: Madrid – at the airport and on the plane

We are now at Madrid airport. The flight to Paris is announced over the loudspeaker system. On his way to the embarkation gate Julio meets another traveller. His name is Manuel Escudero. This casual encounter will have important repercussions later on in the story. During the flight Julio becomes rather talkative and explains to his new acquaintance the reasons for his journey and the nature of his work. He goes into some detail about what he and his firm can do in the field of public transport. Sr. Escudero shows a great deal of interest, but does not say much about himself or his work. At his behest Julio agrees to supply some information. The scene concludes as the aircraft approaches its destination.

LANGUAGE NOTES

17 **El gusto es mío**   *Pleased to meet you too*
A polite reply to the expression (**tanto** or **mucho**) **gusto.**

24 **dos millones de habitantes**   *two million inhabitants*
56 **un millón de personas**   *a million people*
Notice that whenever you use **millón** and state a million what, you must use **de** before the noun.

62 **para que se haga una idea**   *so that you get an idea*
The subjunctive is always used after **para que** (App. M).

59 **¿Le importaría hacerlo?**   *Would you mind doing that?*
64 **Se lo agradecería muchísimo**   *I'd be most grateful to you*
Note the conditionals **importaría** and **agradecería** (App. J).

WORDLIST

se ruega a los pasajeros	passengers are requested
la tarjeta de embarque azul	the blue boarding pass
dirigirse	to make one's way
media hora de retraso	half an hour late
tanto gusto	pleased to meet you
imaginarse	to imagine
la ciudad	city, town
dos millones de habitantes	two million inhabitants
la red de tranvías	streetcar network
aconsejar	to advise
diseñar	to design
hasta	even
montar	to set up
encargarse de	to take charge of
el precio	price
más barato que	more cheaply than
aún	still, yet
particular	private
ofrecer algún negocio	to offer some business
la asesoría de empresas	management consulting
mantener	to maintain
el gobierno	government
la gente	people
alegrarse	to be pleased
el ejemplo	example
el Oriente Medio	Middle East
desde luego que no	of course not
el bosquejo	outline, draft
para que se haga una idea	so that you get an idea
aterrizar	to land
apagar los cigarrillos	to extinguish cigarettes
abrocharse	to fasten
el cinturón de seguridad	safety belt

Cassette 2 Side 1
The new offices in Paris

SCENE 1: Paris – in some empty offices

Luisa and a realtor arrive at a building somewhere in the center of Paris. The realtor is going to show her some offices which are for rent. They talk about the area and then they go up to the floor where the offices are located. The realtor shows her around, pointing out the most relevant features, in the way that realtors do. Luisa enquires about the size and orientation of the rooms, and about the possibility of carrying out some internal alterations. Finally they discuss the rent and length of the lease. There appears to be no problem.

LANGUAGE NOTES

12 **¿Qué tamaño tiene?**   *What size is it?*
25 **¿Cuánto mide?**   *What does it measure?*
Two useful questions here regarding dimensions.

18 **algo de televisión era**   *it was something to do with TV*
Era is part of the imperfect of **ser** (Appendix F).

49 **Depende de lo que quiera hacer**   *It depends on what you want to do*

59 **No creo que sea difícil**   *I don't think it'll be difficult*
Note the subjunctives **quiera,** used after **lo que,** and **sea** (from **ser**), used after **no creo que.** See Appendix M.

WORDLIST

la zona	area
la planta	floor, storey
subir	to go up
el ascensor	elevator
subir a pie	to walk up
el tamaño	size
el metro cuadrado	square metre
el vestíbulo	entrance hall
algo de televisión	something to do with television
era	it was
el wáter	toilet
la cocinita	small kitchen
la sala de reuniones	meeting room
medir (i)	to measure
la ventana	window
¿le da el sol?	does the sun shine into it?
el sur	south
girar	to revolve
el enchufe	socket
¿nos queda algo?	is there anything else?
el tabique	partition
reducir	to reduce
ninguno	none
el permiso	permission
depender de	to depend on
la distribución	layout
el alquiler	rent
por adelantado	in advance
el arriendo	lease
renovar (ue)	to renew
nos sirve	it'll do for us
ultimar	to finalize, conclude
el trámite	transaction

PRACTICE 1: How to describe an office

This section further develops the language of the previous scene concerning office dimensions, facilities and financial arrangements. As usual listen a number of times and repeat in the pauses.

LANGUAGE NOTES

1 **han estado hablando de**   *have been talking about*

23 **¿Va entendiendo lo que dicen?**   *Are you following what they are saying?*
In Spanish the continuous tenses are formed with the appropriate tense of **estar** (or less often **ir** as in the second example) and the gerund. They are not used as often as they are in English.

5 **al entrar**   *as we go in* (literally *on going in*)
Al followed by an infinitive is the equivalent of the English *on* followed by the gerund.

24 **¿Qué extensión tiene?**   *What's the overall size?*
Another useful question relating to dimensions.

42 **Por adelantado**   *In advance*
43 **¿Puedo alquilarlo por tres años?**   *Can I rent it for three years?*
Note the use of **por** in the fixed phrase **por adelantado** and to refer to a fixed period of time.

50 **Julio y Luisa se encuentran en las nuevas oficinas**   *Julio and Luisa are in the new offices*
Encontrarse is an alternative to **estar** when talking about position.

WORDLIST

describir	to describe
al entrar	as we go in
servir (i) de	to serve as
tres metros de lado	three metres long per side
la cocina	kitchen
¿va entendiendo?	are you following …?
la extensión	size
la estación	station
el banco	bank
la tienda	shop
el aparcamiento	parking
la parada de autobús	bus stop
cerca	nearby
la planta baja	ground floor
los bajos	the bottom ones
el franco	franc
al año	a/per year
trimestralmente	every three months
el trimestre	three month period
alquilar	to rent
a los tres años	after three years
claro	clear
encontrarse (ue)	to be, to be found

SCENE 2: Paris – in the new offices

Luisa is in the new offices wondering where Julio is. Julio is looking for Luisa. They seem to have difficulty in coordinating their actions. This time there has been some confusion about the floor the new offices are on. At last they meet and Luisa shows Julio round. She explains how she intends to use the various rooms and points out where she wants the office equipment. Julio is pleasantly impressed, particularly with his own office. He has the task of finding a new secretary. M. Leconte might be able to help. Luisa wants the office to be functioning as soon as possible.

LANGUAGE NOTES

4 **Llevo un rato buscándote** *I've been looking for you for a while*
Note the combination of **llevar** and a gerund: **lleva dos horas preparándolo** *he's been preparing it for two hours.*

13 **Me gusta** *I like it*
Remember that in Spanish you have to say that something pleases you: **le gusta el dinero** *he likes money,* **me gustan las oficinas** *I like the offices.*

14 **me he equivocado de número** *I got the wrong number*
Spanish uses the verb **equivocarse** for a wide range of "wrong" phrases: **me equivoqué** *I was wrong.*

34 **Necesitamos alguien que sepa escribir a máquina** *We need someone who can type*
Note the subjunctive **sepa** from **saber** (Appendix M).

WORDLIST

¿hay alguien?	is there anyone in/there?
por fin	at last
llevo un rato buscándote	I've been looking for you for a while
la luz	light
amplio	spacious
me parece que sí	I think so
equivocarse de	to make a mistake, get wrong
la fotocopiadora	photocopier
planeado	organized, planned
mayor	bigger
cosa de	a matter of
un par de	a couple of, a pair of
darse prisa	to be in a hurry
la recepción	reception
a punto	ready
¿por dónde empezamos?	where do we start?
mandar	to order
lo primero	first of all
sepa	can, knows how to
escribir a máquina	to type
ofrecerse a	to offer to
a ti se te dará bien	you'll be quite happy
elegir (i)	to choose
el acceso	access
el ordenador	computer
en marcha	on the move

PRACTICE 2: Office equipment

Here we have some further practice using terminology useful to the office. As in previous practice sections you learn by listening to two people actually discussing real day to day matters. Listen several times and repeat in the pauses in the usual manner.

LANGUAGE NOTES

2 **las cosas que se encuentran en una oficina**   *the things that are to be found in an office*
Once again we see **encontrarse** being used to refer to place.

5 **una carpeta para cada empresa**   *a folder for every company*

8 **por orden alfabético**   *in alphabetical order*
Some people get a little confused between **para** and **por** because both of them can mean *for*. However it does help if you remember that **por** can also mean *by* or *through* just as often and if you try to memorize useful set phrases like **por orden alfabético** and **por adelantado** *in advance*.

22 **Julio va a ver a M. Leconte para que le ayude a buscar una secretaria**   *Julio is going to see M. Leconte so that he can help him to find a secretary*
Note again the subjunctive **ayude** used after **para que**. Look carefully at the following sentence and compare it with the one in your practice section: **Julio va a ver a M. Leconte para ayudarle a buscar una secretaria** *Julio is going to see M. Leconte to help him find a secretary*. Note too that there is no personal **a** used before **una secretaria.** This is because he is not talking about a particular secretary, just someone who can do the job.

WORDLIST

la carta	letter
el documento	document
el archivo	file
la carpeta	folder
la dirección	address
el fichero	card index, filing cabinet
el orden	order
alfabético	alphabetical
escribir	to write
la fotocopia	photocopy
el cálculo	calculation
la calculadora	calculator

SCENE 3: Paris – in the offices of the holding company

We are now in M. Leconte's office. Julio has come to see if M. Leconte can help them to find a secretary. Julio explains the kind of secretary they are looking for and M. Leconte suggests how they can go about it. It shouldn't be too difficult. But Julio has a second request. He wants to move out of his hotel into an apartment. M. Leconte has an idea that something has been reserved for Julio. He phones a French colleague – M. Bosin – who is in charge of such matters. And yes, there is not one but two apartments reserved in his name! Somebody phoned from Madrid to make the reservations. Who could it have been? Julio seems to know and goes off to see M. Bosin about it.

LANGUAGE NOTES

1 **¿Se puede?**   *May I (come in)?*
This is a useful phrase for asking permission.

11 **¿Tiene que saber idiomas?**   *Must she know languages?*
Notice that **saber,** not **conocer,** is used with languages.

27 **Yo estoy seguro de que le habían reservado algo**
I'm sure that they had reserved something for you
35 **La chica está segura**   *The girl is sure*
Note that in the first sentence the person who is sure is a man, hence **seguro,** in the second it is a girl, hence **segura.** Remember that in Spanish the pluperfect tense is made up of the imperfect of **haber** and a past participle (Appendix I), **habían reservado** *they had reserved.*

WORDLIST

¿se puede?	may I (come in)?
en realidad	in fact
la recepcionista	receptionist
contestar	to answer
¿cosas de esas?	things like that
el caso es que sirva	the point is that he/she should be suitable
la sección de personal	personnel department
cuanto antes mejor	the sooner the better
habían reservado	they had reserved
el alojamiento	accommodation
¡puñetas!	damn!
quién	who
fue	it was
estar de vuelta	to be back

PRACTICE 3: Chats among friends

This section gives you some useful practice in the kind of simple greetings that one exchanges with friends at any time. Added to the greetings you already know you will have a range that will enable you to vary what you say. Follow your usual procedure of listening and repeating.

LANGUAGE NOTES

2 **al verse**   *on meeting*
Here is another example of the use of **al** followed by an infinitive. It can often be translated by *when* so that the translation here could also be *when they meet* or *when they see each other*.

3 **¿Cómo te va?**   *How are you/How's it going?*
4 **Bien. ¿Y a ti?**   *Fine. And you?*
¿Cómo te va? is a handy alternative to **¿Cómo estás?**
The correct way to enquire after the person's state is then **¿Y a ti?** not **¿Y tú?** which is the response to **¿Cómo estás?** or **¿Qué tal?**

5 **¿Marcha todo bien?**   *Is everything going well?*
6 **¿Cómo van los negocios?**   *How's business?*
As you can see both **marchar** and **ir** are used to ask how things are going.
Remember that **los negocios** refer to business in general while **el negocio** is one piece of business.

8 **¿Y los tuyos?**   *And yours?*
12 **¿Y la tuya?**   *And yours?*
Los tuyos refers to **los negocios** (masculine plural) and **la tuya** to **la familia** (feminine singular). (App. R)

WORDLIST

la charla	chat
entre	between, among
decirse	to say to each other
al verse	on meeting
¿cómo te va?	how are you?
¿y a ti?	and you?
voy tirando	I'm getting along
marchar	to go
no hay queja	I can't complain
el jefe	boss
como siempre	as usual
el intercambio	exchange
amistoso	friendly

SCENE 4: Paris – in the central offices of the holding company

Julio gets to M. Bosin's office and is pleased to discover that his secretary speaks Spanish. He has to wait a few minutes until M. Bosin returns. After the introductions Julio hears about the kind of accommodations reserved in his name. Too large and far too expensive. M. Bosin confirms Julio's suspicions as to who the culprit is. It had to be her! Julio explains it has all been a mistake, a misunderstanding. He is looking for something totally different – small and cheap. Not an easy task in Paris, but M. Bosin promises to help.

LANGUAGE NOTES

11 **Siéntese ahí**   *Sit down there*
The **tú** form would of course be **siéntate.**

19 **por lo de los apartamentos**   *about that apartment business*
Note how **lo de** is used in such cases: **lo de los teléfonos**
that problem with the phones.

28 **ha habido una equivocación**   *there's been a mistake*
Ha habido is the perfect tense equivalent of **hay** and **había.**

51 **Haré lo que pueda**   *I'll do what I can*
Haré is part of the future tense of **hacer** (Appendix E).
Lo que is vague, referring to what may have to be done, and so is followed by the subjunctive (Appendix M).

53 **¡Marisa está loca!**   *Marisa is mad!*
If Marisa really were insane Julio would say **es loca.**

WORDLIST

estar a punto de	to be on the point of
sentarse (ie)	to sit down
siento haberle hecho esperar	I'm sorry to have kept you waiting
caro	expensive
al parecer	apparently
el ejecutivo	executive
la renta	rent
ha habido	there has been
la equivocación	mistake
tratarse de	to be about
un error	error, mistake
el malentendido	misunderstanding
barato	cheap
cuanto más pequeño mejor	the smaller the better
el soltero	bachelor
el apartamento de soltero	bachelor apartment
haré	I'll do
lo que pueda	whatever I can
quedar agradecido	to be grateful
loco	mad, crazy

PRACTICE 4: How to clear up a misunderstanding

Julio has been put in a tight spot by Marisa and has had to talk his way out of it. This practice section deals with some of the expressions he has had to use. Listen and repeat as usual.

LANGUAGE NOTES

11 **La renta es más alta**   *The rent is higher*
Remember that **más** is placed in front of an adjective to form the comparative with the definite article added to form the superlative: **la renta es más alta** *the rent is higher,* **la renta es la más alta de París** *the rent is the highest in Paris.*

14 **me había dicho**   *you had told me*
This is another pluperfect tense. Remember **dicho,** the past participle of **decir.**

18 **me temo que no**   *I'm afraid not*
26 **me temo que sí**   *I'm afraid so*
Two useful expressions of regret to have at hand.

28 **Aclarado el error**   *With the error cleared up*
The past participle is often used with a noun in this way: **terminada la fiesta** *the party over,* **firmado el contrato** *with the contract signed.*

WORDLIST

parar los pies	to curb
pasarse	to go too far
el apuro	tight spot, fix
rectificar	to rectify
excusarse	to apologize
alto	high
había dicho	had told
me temo que no	I'm afraid not
seguir (i) adelante	to proceed, move on

SCENE 5: Paris – in the new offices

Julio is back in the new offices conversing with Luisa. Two
more team members have arrived from Barcelona and
Luisa wants Julio to meet them. There is also a letter for
Julio, from his secretary. Julio opens the letter. You hear
the letter read by his secretary with some asides and
interjections by Julio. The letter clarifies the question of
the two apartments and it illustrates further Marisa's
personality and her feelings towards Julio. Eventually
Luisa takes Julio away from his letter and introduces the
two new members, Jaime Tusell and Pablo Ríos, an
accountant and a lawyer. The team is ready to start work.

LANGUAGE NOTES

6 **Voy a presentártelos**   *I'm going to introduce them to you*
Note that the 2nd person pronoun **te** precedes the 3rd **los.**

15 **Los italianos son guapísimos**   *Italian men are very
handsome*
The ending **-ísimo/a** is added to adjectives to intensify the
meaning. The final vowel of the adjective is dropped.

21 **Mi gozo en un pozo**   *I'm sunk*
This idiom literally means *my pleasure in a well.*

44 **Los hombres sois todos iguales**   *You men are all the
same*
Sois is used here because the subject is **(vosotros) los hombres.**

49 **voy a presentaros**   *I'm going to introduce you*
Luisa uses **os** here because she is not talking to all her
colleagues who have to be introduced to each other.

WORDLIST

la línea	line
hace un tiempo ideal	the weather's ideal
poner	to turn, make
moreno	dark, brown
guapísimo	very handsome
tener éxito	to be successful
chiflar	to make one crazy
la suerte	luck
el único	the only one
mi gozo en un pozo	I'm sunk
el sueldo	salary
el rey	king
dejar en paz	to leave in peace
las noticias	news
largo	long
terminar	to finish
la playa	beach
enseñar	to teach
el esquí acuático	waterskiing
igual	same
comportarse	to behave
liarse con	to get involved with
la jefa	boss (female)
fiarse de	to trust
a tu disposición	at your service
las finanzas	finances
el dinero	money
conviene	it's important to
el derecho	law
constituir	to form
el equipo	team
no hay duda	there's no doubt
a trabajar	let's get to work

PRACTICE 5: Introductions

Some excellent practice here concerning introductions –
how to introduce people and what to say when you are
introduced yourself. You'll find one or two expressions to
add to the ones you already know. As usual listen a few
times and then repeat in the pauses.

LANGUAGE NOTES

8 **Encantada de conocerle**   *Pleased to meet you*
16 **Encantado de conocerles**   *Pleased to meet you*
The differences here are slight but important. The first
speaker is a woman and so she says **encantada;** she is also
speaking to one person and hence uses **conocerle.** The
second speaker is a man talking to two or more people and
so he uses **encantado** and **conocerles.**

13 **El gusto es mío**   *Pleased to meet you too*
This polite reply to **tanto gusto** or **mucho gusto** means
literally *the pleasure is mine.*

17 **Hechas las presentaciones**   *With the introductions made*
Here we have another example of the past participle used
with a noun as we saw in Practice 4 with **aclarado el error.**
Hecho is the past participle of **hacer** and you will notice
how it agrees with **presentaciones.**

WORDLIST

el representante	representative
unido	united
el departamento de ventas	sales department
la asesora jurídica	legal consultant
mismo	same
hecho	made
la presentación	introduction
comenzar (ie)	to begin, start

SCENE 6: In the offices in Paris

This scene has three sections. In the first one Julio is talking
to Jaime, the new accountant. He wants Jaime's help to
do some calculations. Do you remember the request for
information made to Julio by someone he met on the
Madrid-Paris flight? It is about that. In the second section
Julio is dictating a couple of letters. One to Sr. Escudero
to send him details and costs as requested. The other
letter goes to Marisa, his secretary in Madrid. But he does
not send it in his name. I wonder why? Finally Julio goes
to Luisa's office to tell her about his dealings with Sr.
Escudero. Julio sounds enthusiastic, but you will detect
some irony in Luisa's words. The situation is not as
promising as Julio thinks. In fact, as you will see, the
opposite is the case.

LANGUAGE NOTES

7   **Eso es lo mío**   *That's my job*
55 **interesado en lo nuestro**   *interested in our affairs*
   Note how **lo** is used with possessives in these sentences.

8   **Hiciste un trabajo**   *You did a job*
   Hiciste is part of the preterite of **hacer** (Appendix H).

24 **Me pidió que le enviase**   *He asked me to send him*
   As **pedir** is used in the preterite tense here, the following
   subjunctive must be imperfect (Appendix L and M).

24 **Estimado señor Escudero**   *Dear Mr Escudero*
   Read through the letters dictated by Julio because they contain
   some useful general phrases for letter writing in Spanish.

60 **Le he escrito**   *I've written to him*
   Escrito is the past participle of **escribir** (Appendix G).

WORDLIST

las cuentas	accounts
algo que ver con	something to do with
Jordania	Jordan
variar	to vary
hasta qué punto	how far
basarse en	to rely on
no ... siquiera	not even
estimado señor	dear Mr
el punto	period
adjunto le remito	I'm enclosing
el caso	matter
ha de	it has to
debido a que	due to the fact that
aparte	new paragraph
a la espera de su respuesta	awaiting your reply
le saluda atentamente	yours sincerely
dirigido	addressed
complacer	to oblige
sin otro particular	nothing else
encontrarse (ue) a	to meet
por casualidad	by chance
¡no me digas!	you don't say!
el nivel	level
gubernamental	government(al)
la competencia	competition
acertado	wise, sensible
cancelar	to cancel
el envío	dispatch, sending

Cassette 2   Side 2
I'm off to Barcelona

SCENE 1: In the offices in Paris

Julio and Luisa meet in the office. They have not seen
each other for two or three days. Luisa has been very
busy, whereas Julio has had little to do. There is not much
work for him. They discuss his schedule for the coming
week. He will be going to Barcelona to attend a meeting
and he will be interviewing applicants for the secretarial
post. That is all. No wonder he is feeling rather low. Luisa
tries to lift his spirits. There will be better times ahead.
But for the time being he can't even accompany Luisa to
the computer centre. He has an interview then.

LANGUAGE NOTES

4   **Hace días que no te veo**   *I haven't seen you for days*
Note how **hace ... que** and the present tense is used, again
describing an event begun in the past and either not
completed or just being completed, as here.

25   **esperando a que suene el teléfono**   *waiting for the phone
to ring*
The subjunctive follows **esperar a que** when you are
waiting for something to happen (Appendix M).

29   **sin hacer nada**   *without doing anything*
Notice the negative effect of **sin: sin ver a nadie** *without
seeing anyone.*

WORDLIST

tener algo entre manos	to have something in hand/ on one's hands
la mano	hand
el periódico	newspaper
programado	arranged, organized
fuera	away
la reunión	meeting
el comité de empresas	business committee
entrevistar	to interview
la chica	girl
el puesto	post
alguna otra cosa	anything else
absolutamente	absolutely
desmoralizante	demoralizing
aburrirse	to get bored
sentado	sitting
todo el día	all day
sonar (ue)	to ring, sound
esperemos que sí	let's hope so
conmigo	with me
¿para qué?	what for?
qué se va a hacer	what's to be done

PRACTICE 1: The agenda for the day

Here you have the chance to practise various ways of asking someone what he/she will be doing during the day and also of answering those questions. It includes using future tense forms and the alternative **ir a.** Follow your normal procedure of listening a number of times and repeating in the pauses.

LANGUAGE NOTES

1 **Luisa y Julio estaban hablando de lo que éste tenía programado** *Luisa and Julio were talking about what the latter had planned*
As you know **éste** means *this (one).* Here it refers to Julio and so naturally we translate it as the *latter.* To refer to Luisa as *the former* we would have used **aquélla.** Hence **éste, ésta** *the latter;* **aquél, aquélla** *the former.*
Note that there is a difference between **tenía programado** and the perfect tense **ha programado** *has planned.* **Tenía programado** indicates that things have been planned but not necessarily by Julio himself. It is a plan that he possesses. You'll see further examples later.

32 **Que descanse** *Let him rest*
Another example of **que** and the subjunctive expressing a wish for someone. Look out for it again later on.

33 **Oigamos** *Let's hear*
The **nosotros** form of the present subjunctive is used to make the suggestion *let's.* Remember **escuchemos** *let's listen to.*

WORDLIST

éste	the latter
el resto	rest
comprobar (ue)	to check
el estado de ventas	sales report
quedar en	to arrange
de vuelta	back
echar una siesta	to have a nap
que descanse	let him rest
descansar	to rest

SCENE 2: In the offices in Paris

In this scene you hear Julio interviewing an applicant. She is an English girl called Linda Bloomfield. She speaks Spanish. Julio offers her a cup of coffee. And he remembers nostalgically the coffee-maker he lost in. Madrid! The interview follows the normal course in such cases. Julio enquires about her command of foreign languages, her typing speed, her knowledge of the work the firm does, etc. He also wants to know about her experience, and the reasons why she wishes to change her job. At the end he promises to let her know their decision as soon as possible.

LANGUAGE NOTES

7   **Llego con adelanto**   *I'm early*
    Con adelanto is the opposite of **con retraso** *late.*

12   **No diría que no**   *I wouldn't say no*
    A useful little phrase. **Diría** is part of the conditional tense of **decir** (Appendix J).

16   **Solo**   *Black*
    This is the normal way to refer to black coffee. **Café con leche** has a lot of milk in it and is usually served in large cups at breakfast. To order coffee with just a little milk ask for **café cortado.**

27   **¿Y cómo anda de mecanografía?**   *And how's your typing?*
    A useful idiom for asking how well someone does something or how they are for something; **¿cómo anda de dinero?** *how are you for money?*

WORDLIST

la entrevista	interview
llegar con adelanto	to arrive early
amable	kind
no diría que no	I wouldn't say no
la leche	milk
el azúcar	sugar
solo	black (of coffee)
el gerente	manager
exportar	to export
el contacto	contact
¿cómo anda de ...?	how's your ...?
la mecanografía	typing
la taquigrafía	shorthand
a máquina	on the typewriter
dar cincuenta pulsaciones	to tap out fifty characters
el informe	report
la mecanógrafa	typist
solo	alone
por mi cuenta	on my account
referirse (ie) a	to refer to
la industria del transporte	transport industry
a fines de	at the end of
lo antes posible	as soon as possible

PRACTICE 2: Interviews

This practice section centres on an interview for a job. It enables you to practise some useful expressions and phrases which you can adapt to talk about yourself. Listen several times and repeat in the pauses.

LANGUAGE NOTES

29 **¿Cuántos años lleva trabajando?**   *How many years have you been working?*
This is another way of expressing time spent doing something. A full answer to the question could be **llevo dos años trabajando** *I've been working for two years.*

30 **Trabajé en una empresa durante tres años**   *I worked in a company for three years*
When *for* indicates during a period of time the normal Spanish word to use is **durante** which also means *during.*

44 **Pregúntele si tiene hijos**   *Ask him if he's got children*
Hijo *son* is also used, especially in the plural, to refer to children.

46 **si le gusta viajar**   *if he likes travelling*
Remember how to express liking in Spanish by using **gusta** or **gustan** according to what is liked: **me gusta el café** *I like coffee* , **me gustan los puros** *I like cigars.* When you refer to liking doing something you use **gusta** with the infinitive, as here in **le gusta viajar.**

WORDLIST

valer	to be OK
el título	qualification
el certificado	certificate
el diploma	diploma
los estudios empresariales	business studies
el instituto	institute, college
durante	for, during
estar parado	to be unemployed
cuál	which, what
último	last
la compañía de seguros	insurance company
el agente de seguros	insurance agent
el hijo	child, son
la cafetería	café, cafeteria

SCENE 3: Paris – in a café

Julio and Luisa are having lunch together. In the background you hear the normal noises in a French café. Julio wants to get to know Luisa better. She looks too young to be in such a responsible post. Mixing flattery and boldness he asks some very personal questions about her age and about her private life. She doesn't seem to mind. Then the conversation drifts toward matters concerned with work – Luisa's visit to the computer centre and Julio's interviews. It looks as if Miss Bloomfield will be the new secretary. The decision is left in Julio's hands.

LANGUAGE NOTES

17 **Tal vez haya tenido suerte**   *Perhaps I've been lucky*
We have here the perfect subjunctive, made up of the present tense of **haber** and the past participle.

28 **No los aparentas**   *You don't look it*
The **los** refers to **treinta y tres años.**

28 **¿No has pensado nunca en casarte?**   *Haven't you ever thought about getting married?*
There's another double negative here in **no ... nunca.** **Casarse** means *to marry, get married* and refers to the act itself. Note that you use **con** when you mention the person someone is married to: **se casó con María** *he married María*. Notice the difference with **estar casado** which indicates the state of being married: **estuve casada** (30).

48 **Ya se lo dije**   *I did tell her about it*

WORDLIST

se come bien y barato	you can eat well and cheaply
joven	young
al frente de	in charge of
la impertencia	cheek, impertinence
qué va	of course not, nonsense
la responsabilidad	responsibility
raro	unusual
tener suerte	to be lucky
la colega	colleague (female)
aparentar	to appear, look
pensar (ie) en	to think about
casarse	to get married
salir bien	to turn out well
acordarse (ue) de	to remember
¿nos sirve?	will she suit us?
la personalidad	personality
estar acostumbrado	to be used to
muchas veces	often
cuanto antes	as soon as possible

PRACTICE 3: Listen in order to understand (2)

This is another practice section in which we want you to listen carefully in order to pick up the general drift of the conversation. Listen a number of times before looking at the text in your book and at the vocabulary and language notes. Finally listen again and repeat in the pauses.

LANGUAGE NOTES

5 **No recuerdo**   *I don't remember*
   Recordar is an alternative to **acordarse.**

6 **verás qué bien sabe**   *you'll see how nice it tastes*
   Saber also means *to taste:* **sabe a ajo** *it tastes like garlic.*

7 **¿Qué lleva?**   *What's in it?*
   Note the new meaning of **llevar** here referring to ingredients.

13 **me gustaría organizar una fiesta**   *I'd like to organize a party*
   Me gustaría, the conditional form of **me gusta,** is a polite way of saying you want something or to do something.

24 **Voy a llamar al camarero para que nos traiga uno a cada una**
   I'm going to call the waiter so that he can bring us one each
   Remember that the subjunctive always follows **para que, traiga** being part of the subjunctive of **traer.**
   Cada una is a feminine form because the two customers are female. Had they been male **cada uno** would have been used.

WORDLIST

seguro que sí	I'm sure
creo que no	I don't think so
saber	to taste
¿qué lleva?	what's in it?
el jugo	juice
la naranja	orange
fuerte	strong
me gustaría	I'd like
el cóctel	cocktail
volver (ue) loco	to drive mad
el ambiente	atmosphere
los años veinte	the twenties
la música	music
vestido con	dressed in
atreverse	to dare
venga	let's have it
el camarero	waiter
uno a cada una	one each
la bebida	drink

SCENE 4: In the offices in Paris

Julio is on the phone. His conversation is coming to an end as Luisa walks in. He has just offered Miss Bloomfield the job of secretary. Luisa has a letter in her hand. An invitation to attend an exposition in Barcelona. Something connected with their work. Since Julio is going to Barcelona he might as well visit the exposition. He does not like some of the arrangements, but Luisa will ease matters by putting him in touch with someone at her old company. Luisa used to work for DATASA in Barcelona. Finally, Julio is on the phone again, booking a flight to Barcelona. One of his two last names is rather unusual and it creates a slight problem.

LANGUAGE NOTES

9 **¿De qué se trata?**   *What's it about?*
A very useful question to remember.

12 **Hotel Colón**
Colón is the Spanish for *Columbus.* There is a famous monument to Columbus overlooking Barcelona harbour.

13 **De la I.M.C.**
You'll learn all about the Spanish alphabet in the next practice section.

17 **Demasiado técnico para mí**   *Too technical for me*
Demasiado can also mean *too much:* **come demasiado** *he eats too much,* **bebe demasiada cerveza** *he drinks too much beer.*

WORDLIST

¿de qué se trata?	what's it about?
la invitación	invitation
el sistema	system
integrado	integrated
es cosa tuya	that's your area
demasiado	too
el asistente	person present
merecer la pena	to be worth the effort
mandar	to send
me va muy bien	that suits me fine

PRACTICE 4: The alphabet in Spanish

It is very useful to know the names of the letters in the Spanish alphabet as you never know when you might have to spell out your name or address. Remember you can't offer to write it out if you're on the phone. Listen a few times and repeat the letters in the pauses. Practise until you can go right through the Spanish alphabet. Then spell out the names of the cities in the pauses. Finally make sure you can spell out your own name, the names of your family, address etc.

LANGUAGE NOTES

3 **a, b, c, ch**
Note that **ch** is considered a separate letter, following **c**.

5 **una sola letra**   *a single letter*
Here's another meaning for **solo**. **Letra** is reserved for letters of the alphabet, **carta** is used for correspondence.

8 **l, ll, m**
Double **ll** is also considered to be a separate letter.

10 **n, ñ, o**
The mark over **ñ** is called a tilde. This is also a separate letter.

17 **L mayúscula**   *Capital l*
The opposite of **mayúscula** is **minúscula**.

WORDLIST

el alfabeto	alphabet
sencillo	simple
deletrear	to spell
considerarse	to be considered
solo	single
la letra	letter (of alphabet)
fijarse	to notice
doble	double
la tilde	tilde (-)
Londres	London
la mayúscula	capital letter
Sevilla	Seville

SCENE 5: Barcelona – in the hotel

The scene takes place at the hotel reception in Barcelona. The conversation is between Julio and the night porter. Julio's flight was delayed and he arrives rather late at the hotel. He had reserved a room from Paris, but the night porter cannot find any record of the reservation. And he is not particularly helpful either. The conversation takes on sharp tones. Poor Julio is even forced to pay for the room in advance. His visit to Barcelona does not have a very good start.

LANGUAGE NOTES

1 **Buenas**   *Good evening*
Buenas tardes and **buenas noches** are often shortened in speech to **buenas,** likewise **buenos días** to **buenos.**

3 **La tengo reservada**   *I've got one reserved*
This is another example of **tener** and a past participle. Note the difference: **he reservado una habitación** *I've reserved a room,* **tengo reservada una habitación** *I've got a room reserved.*

5 **Julio Gómez Huidobro**
Like all Spaniards Julio has two last names. **Gómez** is his father's name, **Huidobro** his mother's. He will be known as **Gómez.** A married woman replaces her mother's name with her husband's first surname. Hence if Julio married Rosa Ruiz Marcos her married name would be **Rosa Ruiz (de) Gómez.**

WORDLIST

buenas	good evening, good night
el portero	porter, doorman
a nombre de	in the name of
a causa de	because of
confirmar	to confirm
a ese nombre	in that name
individual	single
el baño	bath, bathroom
la ducha	shower
después de	after
medianoche	midnight
el pago	payment
hasta por la mañana	until the morning
sólo estoy yo	there's only me
tenga	here you are
vaya hotel	what a hotel
el piso	floor

PRACTICE 5: On arriving at the hotel

When you check into a Spanish hotel, not having made a reservation in advance, you need to be able not only to state your requirements but to ask questions about the accommodations. This section enables you to get some practice in this area. As usual listen several times. Take note of what the man in the hotel says and then, instead of repeating in the pauses, take his part.

LANGUAGE NOTES

13 **O diciéndolo todo junto**   *Or saying it all together*
The instruction here is for the speaker to put into one sentence what his requirements are. **Diciendo** is the gerund of **decir** (Appendix B).

17 **¿Cuánto cuesta?**   *How much does it cost?*
One of the most useful and important questions to know.

19 **lo que incluye el precio**   *what the price includes*
¿Está incluido el desayuno?   *Is breakfast included?*
Note the **y** in the present tense forms **incluyo, incluyes, incluye, incluyen** and in the gerund **incluyendo**.

22 **¿Da a la calle?**   *Does it overlook the street?*
Try to adapt this question to ask if a room overlooks:
the beach (**la playa**), *the swimming pool* (**la piscina**), *the garden* (**el jardín**), *the courtyard* (**el patio**), *the park* (**el parque**), *the mountains* (**las montañas**).

25 **Quiere que le despierten**   *He wants them to wake him*
Remember the use of the subjunctive with **querer** (App. M).

WORDLIST

quedarse	to stay
para él solo	just for himself
todo junto	all together
costar (ue)	to cost
incluir	to include
incluido	included
el desayuno	breakfast
dar a	to overlook
la calle	street
despertar (ie)	to wake up
levantarse	to get up
atender a	to attend to

SCENE 6: Barcelona – at the conference hall

The scene begins with Julio arriving at the exposition. He is speaking to one of the receptionists. The receptionist indicates that someone is expecting him. It is the contact that Luisa had arranged from Paris. Julio introduces himself to the new man, Fermín Díaz. They have the usual exchanges in these cases: the trip, the hotel, work, and ... Luisa. They both seem rather fond of her. On the other hand, the exposition is only an excuse to take a day off. Suddenly Julio sees a familiar face in the crowd. It is Sr. Escudero. He goes over to him.

LANGUAGE NOTES

8 **aquel señor de azul**   *that man in blue*
36 **el del traje marrón**   *the one in the brown suit*
Note the use of **de** in these phrases.

25 **nada de nuevo**   *nothing new*
Nada is followed by **de** in phrases like this.

28 **lo de siempre**   *the usual (thing/s)*
You can use this to order your usual drink.

41 **Trató de engañarme**   *He tried to trick me*
Be careful not to confuse **tratar de** *to try to* with **tratarse de** *to be about* which we saw in **¿de qué se trata?**

45 **¿Me permite un momento?**   *Can you spare me a moment?*
This is a polite way of asking someone if you can have a word with him/her.

WORDLIST

la tarjeta de identificación	identity card
de azul	dressed in blue
recibir	to welcome
dormir (ue)	to sleep
¿sigue tan guapa como siempre?	is she as pretty as ever?
trabajador	hard working
la exposición	exposition
nada de nuevo	nothing new
la publicidad	publicity
lo de siempre	the usual thing
perder (ie) el tiempo	to waste time
merendar (ie)	to have an afternoon snack
el del traje marrón	the one in the brown suit
el traje	suit
marrón	brown
la cara me es conocida	I know the face
ya caigo	now I remember
engañar	to trick
como lo oyes	just as I'm telling you
¿me permite un momento?	can you spare me a moment?
sabremos	we shall know

Cassette 3   Side 1
Design engineer wanted

SCENE 1: Barcelona – at the conference hall

This scene has two settings. In the first one Julio confronts Sr. Escudero with his deceitful behaviour. Sr. Escudero thinks he did nothing wrong – normal business practice. Julio threatens Sr. Escudero and is on the point of becoming violent. Fermín tries to calm things down from the sidelines. Eventually Fermín succeeds in taking Julio away. Under the circumstances a drink seems advisable, but the bar at the Conference Hall is closed. They go out to find a place to have a beer. And after the beer, why not make an evening of it?

LANGUAGE NOTES

2 **Quisiera hablar**   *I'd like to speak*
It is just that much more polite to use **quisiera** *I'd like* than **quiero** *I want*.

4 **usted dirá**   *what can I do for you?* (lit: *you will say*)

6 **Claro que me acuerdo**   *Of course I remember*
Note **claro que** here and also **¡claro!** *of course!*, **claro que sí** *of course*, **claro que no** *of course not*.

8 **¿Cómo no me dijo …?**   *Why didn't you tell me …?*
Dijo is part of the preterite of **decir;** other irregular preterites here are **hice** *I made*, **estuve** *I was*, **puso** *he put*.

WORDLIST

el palacio de congresos	conference hall
quisiera	I'd like
usted dirá	what can I do for you?
claro que	of course
oportuno	appropriate
sacar información	to get information
hacerse pasar por	to pass oneself off as
hacer preguntas	to ask questions
el cínico	cynic
merecer	to deserve
romper la cara	to punch in the face
tranquilizarse	to calm down
hundir	to ruin
quedarse en la calle	to be out in the street
habrá que verlo	that remains to be seen
andarse con cuidado	to tread carefully
a qué viene todo esto	what all this is leading to
tropezarse	to bump into each other
reaccionar	to react
cerrado	closed
antojarse	to want, feel like
la pérdida	waste
poner cara	to have a look on one's face
dar	to hit, thump
la caña	(glass of) beer
a tu salud	cheers, good health
divertirse (ie)	to enjoy oneself

PRACTICE 1: Having a drink in a bar

It's always enjoyable to visit a bar in Spain to sample the wine and some of the delicious snacks that are available. Here you can practise some of the language useful on such an occasion. Listen a few times to the speakers and then repeat in the pauses.

LANGUAGE NOTES

6 **Muy buenas**   *Good evening*
This can be used as an alternative to **buenas tardes** or **buenas noches.**

14 **Tónica con ginebra**   *Gin and tonic*
More and more in Spain you now hear **un gin tonic.**

16 **algún pincho**   *some snack*
Spanish bars are renowned for the amazing array of snacks or appetizers that they have, ranging from simple nuts and olives to tasty omelettes, fish, hams, sausages etc.

21 **¿Me cambia?**   *Have you got change?*
Another useful question of this type is **¿Me enciende?** *Have you got a light?*

24 **Trescientas veinte pesetas**   *Three hundred and twenty pesetas*
Remember that the numbers from **doscientos** to **novecientos** are considered to be adjectives and have to agree accordingly with the noun.

27 **Esperemos que Julio no haya bebido mucho**   *Let's hope that Julio hasn't drunk a lot*
Remember: **esperar** can mean *to hope, to wait for, to expect.*

WORDLIST

muy buenas	good afternoon/evening
tinto	red (of wine)
seco	dry
dulce	sweet
la tónica con ginebra	gin and tonic
el pincho	snack
la tortilla	omelette
el cigarrillo	cigarette
la moneda	coin, small change
¿me cambia?	have you got change?

SCENE 2: Barcelona – in the offices of DATASA

Fermín and Julio meet "the morning after the night before". They are both feeling rather fragile. Julio has to address a meeting of DATASA executives to explain the work they are doing in Paris. But first he must take something to clear his head. Julio is called into the meeting by Sr. Tuñón; Fermín does the introduction and then Julio begins to explain the Paris project. Their main function is going to be to coordinate from Paris the know-how and technological expertise of all the various companies in the holding. The chief designers from the various companies will have to meet once a month. Sr. Tuñón does not think much of the latter proposal and opposes it. Julio is disappointed with the lack of cooperation.

LANGUAGE NOTES

3 **¿Cómo te encuentras?**   *How do you feel?*
This is a useful alternative to **¿cómo estás?** or **¿cómo te sientes?** in circumstances like these.

12 **Tengo un dolor de cabeza**   *I've got a headache*
Note other examples like this of expressing ailments: **tengo dolor de estómago** *I've got a stomachache*, **tengo dolor de garganta** *I've got a sore throat*. **Un** can be omitted.

16 **Ya voy, ya voy**   *I'm coming, I'm coming*
Spanish speakers often use **ir** *to go* when we use *to come*.

76 **yo esperaba que ustedes se mostrasen**   *I was hoping you'd be*
Note the imperfect subjunctive here after **esperaba que.**

WORDLIST

la resaca	hangover
los demás	others, rest
de al lado	next door
el dolor de cabeza	headache
llevarse	to take away, carry off
establecer	to establish
la base	base, basis
bajo	under
la dirección	direction
el procedimiento	procedure
la especie	kind, sort
la investigación	research
una vez recogida y ordenada esta información	once this information has been gathered and put into order
contactar con	to get in touch with
el avance tecnológico	technological advance
el municipio	town
de segunda mano	second hand
desarrollar	to develop
la tecnología	technology
la esfera	sphere
el comité de enlace	liaison committee
el jefe de diseño	head designer
reunirse	to meet
intercambiar	to exchange
mantenerse al día	to keep up date
lo acordado	what's been agreed
acordar (ue)	to agree
sumo	extreme
el técnico diseñador	design engineer
mensual	monthly
de vez en cuando	from time to time
mostrarse (ue)	to appear

PRACTICE 2: How to state your case

Following on from Julio's disappointing time at the
conference hall, this section deals with two people who are
explaining the same details as Julio. Listen a few times as
usual, paying particular attention to what the woman says.
Then, in the pauses, instead of repeating what the man
says take the woman's part, responding to his comments.

LANGUAGE NOTES

3 **Aunque les expuso la situación muy bien** *Although he
explained the situation very well*
Expuso is part of the preterite of **exponer** which follows
the pattern for **poner** in all tenses, as does **suponer**.

19 **Habrá que celebrar una reunión** *There will have to be
a meeting*
Don't forget that **habrá** is the future form of **hay**.

21 **Diga quién tiene que asistir** *Say who has to attend*
Notice that **asistir** means *to attend* or *be present* and has
nothing to do with assisting or helping: **asistí a la reunión**
I went to/attended the meeting.

29 **Volvamos a París con Julio** *Let's go back to Paris with
Julio*
Remember that one way of expressing *let's* in Spanish is to
use the first person plural **(nosotros)** form of the present
subjunctive: **oigamos** *let's hear*, **escuchemos** *let's listen*,
esperemos *let's hope*.

WORDLIST

exponer	to explain, set out
el caso	case, subject
centralizar	to centralize
coordinar	to coordinate
la misión	mission
asistir	to attend
el detalle	detail
más adelante	later on
un poquillo más	a little more, just a bit more

SCENE 3: In the offices in Paris

Julio is in Paris once again. He is back at the office talking to Ana María, an administrative assistant. There is a telex waiting for him. Marisa, his beloved secretary, is coming to Paris! Julio wants to stop her and decides to send her an urgent telex. He is so shocked he can't even find the right words. And Ana María is not very familiar with the telex machine. Will it arrive in time?

LANGUAGE NOTES

5 **No sé dónde lo he puesto**   *I don't know where I've put it*
Puesto is the past participle of **poner** and as you can see is irregular. You've already come across some other irregular ones like **hecho** (from **hacer**) and **dicho** (from **decir**). See Appendix G.

28 **Ponle ... "No vengas a París"**   *Add to it ... "Don't come to Paris"*

34 **Y ahora dile**   *And now tell her*
Julio addresses both Ana María and Marisa as **tú**. Hence he uses the **tú** command forms **pon** (from **poner**) and **di** (from **decir**) instead of the **usted** forms **ponga** and **diga**. Remember that a negative **tú** command is given by using the present subjunctive as in **no vengas**. The **tú** command for **venir** is **ven**. The negative forms of **pon** and **di** are **no pongas** and **no digas** (Appendix C).

42 **hasta que yo te avise**   *until I tell you*
Note the use of the subjunctive after **hasta que**.

WORDLIST

lo he puesto	I've put it
¡válgame el cielo!	heaven help me!
inmediatamente	immediately
la guía	directory, guide
a la izquierda	on/to the left
personal	personal
urgente	urgent
ponle	add to it
el carácter	character, nature
dile	tell her
nombrar	to appoint
cierto	true
lo último	the last part
añadir	to add
hasta que	until
apretar (ie)	to press
el botón	button
a la derecha	on/to the right
a ver	I wonder

PRACTICE 3: To the right, to the left

A little bit of practice here in the language you need to
point out the differences between driving in Great Britain
and in Spain. As usual, listen a few times until you've
grasped the gist of the conversation and then repeat in the
pauses.

LANGUAGE NOTES

1   **a tiempo**   *on time*
Note that in Spanish you use **a,** not **en.** One of the main
difficulties in learning another language is that so often
the prepositions used in various phrases are not the ones
you might expect. Look out for this as you work through
the course and memorize the phrases that you consider of
particular use to you.

10   **con el volante al otro lado**   *with the steering wheel on the
other side*

12   **¿Por dónde se conduce en Inglaterra?**   *On which side
does one drive in England?*

13   **Por la izquierda**   *On the left*
In the previous scene you encountered **a la izquierda** and **a
la derecha,** yet here we find **por.** Very often **por** indicates
movement as you can see in the question **¿por dónde?** This
kind of usage underlines what we said in the first note.

14   **Por eso el conductor se sienta**   *Therefore the driver sits*
Notice that **conductor** means *driver.* Such words we call
amigos falsos *false friends.*

24   **la mano izquierda**   *the left hand*
Both **izquierdo** and **derecho** are normal adjectives
agreeing with the noun they describe: **el brazo derecho** *the
right arm.*

WORDLIST

preocupado	worried
el ejercicio	exercise
la posición	position
el volante	steering wheel
al otro lado	on the other side
¿por dónde?	on which side?
conducir	to drive
por la izquierda	on the left
por eso	therefore
el conductor	driver
por la derecha	on the right
cambiar velocidades	to shift gears
izquierdo	left
derecho	right
la preocupación	worry

SCENE 4: In the offices in Paris

Julio is muttering to himself thinking that Marisa may walk in at any moment. But Luisa is the one who arrives. She has seen the famous telex and pulls Julio's leg about it. Work and personal relationships do not usually mix well, she thinks. Then Julio shows Luisa an advertisement he has seen in the paper. It is for a job in Caracas. A job that would suit Julio quite well. After all, he does not feel very settled in Paris. He wants to know what Luisa thinks of it.

LANGUAGE NOTES

2 **Marisa se presenta diciendo** *Marisa will appear saying*
23 **Lo vi en el periódico viniendo de Barcelona** *I saw it in the paper coming from Barcelona*
Both **diciendo** and **viniendo** are gerunds and you will notice that in each case the **e** in **decir** and **venir** has changed to **i.** The same thing happens, as you may already have noticed with **pidiendo** and **sirviendo.**

14 **Diciéndole que se quede en Madrid** *Telling her to stay in Madrid*
When you tell someone to do something in Spanish the second verb is in the subjunctive: **dile que vaya a Barcelona** *tell him to go to Barcelona.*

46 **Es cosa tuya** *That's your affair/That's up to you*
You've seen this phrase before. It's used to indicate that something is very much your business; **es cosa mía** *that's my business.*

WORDLIST

seguro que	for certain
cariño	love, darling
hablar solo	to talk to oneself
la semana pasada	last week
querido	beloved, dear
el aviso	message
aconsejable	advisable
mezclar	to mix
la relación	relation(ship)
que lo digas	you can say that again
echar una mirada	to have a look
se requiere	wanted
amplio	wide, broad
avanzado	advanced
la sede	headquarters
la remuneración	salary
gratuito	free
habrá	there will be
dentro de poco	in a little while
es cosa tuya	that's your affair
el informe	reference
apoyar	to support, back

PRACTICE 4: How to describe a job

This section is concerned with working out the details of a job advertisement. The woman is explaining to the man what the company needs and what the salary and conditions will be. The man then places the advertisement in the paper and answers the various questions the newspaper employee puts to him. Listen very carefully as usual and then repeat the woman's questions in the pauses.

LANGUAGE NOTES

16 **Voy a llamar al periódico**   *I'm going to call the paper*
Remember that in Spanish you always call *to* someone or something. The same would apply if **telefonear** were used.

40 **vamos a averiguar las razones por las que Julio quiere cambiar de empleo**   *and now let's find out the reasons why Julio wants to change jobs*
las razones por las que   *the reasons for which*
The **las que** refers to **las razones**.
Remember that you add **de** to **cambiar** when talking about exchanging one thing for another, such as offices, jobs, homes etc.

WORDLIST

la vacante	vacancy
la electrónica	electronics
basado	based
la sección de empleos	jobs section
el tipo	kind, type
el conocimiento	knowledge
el especialista	specialist
dispuesto a	ready to, prepared to
mínimo	minimum
la razón	reason

SCENE 5: In the offices in Paris

The dialogue between Luisa and Julio continues. They are talking about Julio applying for a job in Venezuela. It is understandable. Julio is feeling rather low. His trip to Barcelona was not a success. He tells Luisa about it. Sr. Tuñón in particular proved most uncooperative. But Luisa is not one to be put off by such obstacles. That is why she got to the top so young. She is soon on the phone to DATASA in Barcelona. First, she speaks to the managing director, Sr. Lorca, and then to Tuñón himself. The problem is solved. Julio is most impressed and is beginning to change his mind about the job in Caracas. Besides, Luisa is so attractive ... How about dinner tonight? But no, she can't or she doesn't want to. Maybe she really thinks one should not mix work and personal relationships.

LANGUAGE NOTES

1 ¿**No te sientes a gusto ...?**   *Don't you feel at ease ...?*
Don't confuse **sentirse** *to feel* and **sentarse** to sit down.

12 **no conseguimos llegar a un acuerdo sobre lo del comité de enlace**   *we didn't manage to come to an agreement about that liaison committee business*
Notice once again the use of **lo de** which refers to the matter under discussion, literally *that of*.

33 **Oiga, me pone con ...**   *Hello, put me through to ...*
This is a most useful expression to know when you make a phone call and have to go through the switchboard at the other end.

WORDLIST

sentirse (ie) a gusto	to feel at ease
¿qué tal te fue?	how did you get on?
malísimo	very bad
para colmo	to top it off
conseguir (i)	to manage
el acuerdo	agreement
tal cosa	such a thing
un tal Tuñón	one Tuñón
el tío	character, guy
las gafas	glasses
no lo voy a conocer	of course I do
resolver (ue)	to solve, sort out
poner con	to put through to
asegurarse	to make sure
felicitar	to congratulate
de mi lado	on my side
ceder	to give way
el director gerente	the managing director
no vayas a pensar	don't go thinking
estar contento	to be happy
se me ocurre una idea	I've got an idea
la revista	review
atraer	to attract
¡qué pena!	what a pity!
otra vez será	there'll be another time

PRACTICE 5: Talking about a trip

It's always nice to be able to tell people about trips you have made. Here you can listen to a woman telling a man about her recent visit to London. There are many useful phrases in this section which you can not only learn as models but also easily adapt for your own use. Listen carefully as usual and then repeat in the pauses.

LANGUAGE NOTES

7 **Fuimos a Londres**   *We went to London*
13 **¿Fue un viaje de negocios?**   *Was it a business trip?*
   You will remember that **ir** and **ser** have the same forms in the preterite tense (Appendix H).

8 **Era la primera vez que íbamos**   *It was the first time we went*
   Era and **íbamos** are forms of the imperfect of **ser** and **ir** respectively. They are two of only three irregular ones, the other being **ver** (Appendix F).

9 **Paramos en un hotel pequeño**   *We stayed at a small hotel*
   You may well have noticed that the **nosotros** form of the preterite tense of verbs ending in **-ar** and **-ir** is the same as the present tense. The context will make it clear if one is talking about the present or the past.

23 **¿Os gustaron?**   *Did you like them?*
   As he uses **os** the man is clearly asking the woman about the people she was with as well as about herself.

25 **Regresamos a casa el sábado**   *We returned home on Saturday*
   Notice: **a casa** *home(ward)* involving motion, **en casa** *at home*.
   fuimos a casa *we went home*   **estaba en casa** *I was at home*

WORDLIST

íbamos	we went
parar	to stay, stop
buenísimo	very good
el viaje de negocios	business trip
salir	to go out
un par de veces	a couple of times
¿os gustaron?	did you like them?
regresar a casa	to return home

SCENE 6: In the offices in Paris

Julio does not give up easily. She said no, but ... He goes
to her office to reiterate his invitation. If not dinner, why
not a drink after work? Ana María comes in. There is a
telephone message for Luisa. It is from M. Leconte, and
very personal indeed. The phone rings again. Luisa
answers and Ana María directs her attention towards
Julio. Is she showing some interest in Julio or just trying to
console him? The phone call was not from M. Leconte. It
was from Marisa. She is on her way. Another shock for
Julio!

LANGUAGE NOTES

4 **No tengo nada que hacer**   *I've got nothing to do*
Both **nada** and **algo** are followed by **que** in expressions like
this: **algo que comer** *something to eat.*

13 **estaba pensando en lo de esta noche**   *I've been thinking
about tonight*
Note yet again the use of **lo de,** not translated here, but
referring to something they've already talked about.

16 **es una pena que no podamos salir juntos**   *it's a pity we
can't go out together*
19 **podríamos ir a tomar algo al salir del trabajo**   *we could
go and have something when we leave work*
Salir can be translated as *to go out* or *to leave* as
you can see in these two sentences.
Note the subjunctive after **es una pena que.**

WORDLIST

ganas de	a desire to
nada que hacer	nothing to do
contar (ue) con	to count on
la pena	shame, pity
pasar por	to come to, stop in at
recoger	to pick up, collect
ponerse	to put on, wear
el vestido	dress
llevarse	to get along
estar en camino	to be on the way
meterse	to hide

Cassette 3   Side 2
And now to Rome

SCENE 1: Paris – in a café

Luisa finds Julio sitting in a quiet corner of a café. He seems to be hiding from somebody. Marisa is his main concern. She has decided to come to Paris and he is not very happy about it. But Luisa brings him good news. If he is off to Caracas there is little point in Marisa coming to Paris. Julio's mood changes radically. Suddenly, he feels like celebrating. However, Luisa cannot join him. She has a previous engagement with Antoine. Julio's euphoria fizzles away with the same rapidity.

LANGUAGE NOTES

23 **Yo le dije que suspendiese el viaje**   *I told her to put off the journey*

28 **no merecía la pena que viniese**   *it wasn't worth her while coming*
Note that the two subjunctives here are imperfect as they depend on verbs which are in past tenses.

35 **me gustas más que nunca**   *I like you more than ever*
Julio says literally *you please me more than ever* and this explains why **gustas** is used. Talking to someone else about Luisa he might say **me gusta más que nunca** *I like her more than ever*. More about **gustar** in the next practice section.

44 **No me gusta ni el nombre**   *I don't even like the name*

WORDLIST

el rincón	corner
esconderse	to hide (oneself)
puñetero	damned
justo	fair
la consecuencia	consequence
equivocarse	to be wrong
el zumo	(fresh) juice
me gusta con locura	I love it
suspender	to put off
convencer	to convince
genial	brilliant
estupendo	fantastic
no te pases	don't overdo it
no ... ni	not ... even
tonterías	nonsense
que lo pases bien	have a nice time

PRACTICE 1: I like it very much

Expressing likes and dislikes is something we do every day. As you know **gustar** is used for this purpose in Spanish and this section is devised to give you some practice in using it. You will remember that it is used in a somewhat different way from *like* in English. Listen to the scene carefully to grasp the sense of what is being said and when you are ready repeat in the pauses as usual.

LANGUAGE NOTES

5 **no me gusta este traje**   *I don't like this suit*
Remember that in Spanish the object liked (or disliked), here **el traje,** is the subject of the sentence and what you actually say is that something is pleasing to you. Hence here the man is saying that the suit is not pleasing to him. That is why the verb form is **gusta.** It also explains why he says **¿Y a ti?** *Do you?* lit: *And to you (is it pleasing)?*

11 **Pues a mí me gusta**   *Well I like it*
12 **A mí no**   *I don't*
Using **a mí** in these two comments makes them more emphatic.

12 **No me gustan los colores oscuros**   *I don't like dark colours*
This time the verb is **gustan** because the woman is saying that dark colours are not pleasing to her. Look at some more examples of **gustar: no me gustó el vino** *I didn't like the wine,* **me gustaron las uvas** *I liked the grapes,* **me gustaba el fútbol** *I used to like soccer,* **no me gustaban los gatos** *I didn't use to like cats.*
Notice that in Spanish you use the definite article when you talk about something in a general sense, as above with **los colores oscuros, el fútbol** and **los gatos.**

WORDLIST

el verbo	verb
cierto	certain
la peculiaridad	peculiarity
aquél	that one
gris	grey
oscuro	dark
el color	colour
la variedad	variety
el estilo	style
probarse (ue)	to try on
¿qué te parece?	what do you think of it?
me entusiasma	I like it very much
encontrar (ue)	to find
de su gusto	to their liking

SCENE 2: In the offices in Paris

Luisa meets the new secretary, Linda Bloomfield, the girl
interviewed by Julio. They talk about him. He has gone to
Rome to visit one of the firms they have connections with.
Luisa explains to Linda the nature of the work she has to
do. She introduces her to the various members of the
team. She shows her around the office. And, finally, she
identifies herself as the person in charge.

LANGUAGE NOTES

9 **no está mal**   *that's not bad*
You always use **estar**, not **ser**, with both **mal** and **bien**.

9 **Supongo que no conoces a nadie todavía**   *I suppose you
don't know anyone yet*
Notice that the personal **a** is used with **nadie** as well as
with specific people.

11 **Al señor Gómez que fue el que me entrevistó**
Sr. Gómez who was the one who interviewed me
Linda is saying that she knows Sr. Gómez so although she
leaves out **conozco** the personal **a** is still present in **al**.

20 **No he oído hablar de ella**   *I haven't heard of it*
Ella refers to **la compañía FITA**.

44 **¿Quieres que te las muestre?**   *Do you want me to show
them to you?*
Note that **te** will always precede **lo, la, le, los, las** or **les**.

WORDLIST

lejos	far away
desde	from
estar camino de	to be on the way to
especializarse	to specialize
los ferrocarriles	railways
la tracción	traction
oír hablar de	to hear of
claro está	obviously
ponerse en contacto con	to get in touch with
diverso	different, various
el país	country
necesario	necessary
la rutina	routine
la semana que viene	next week
aumentar	to increase, grow
el contable	accountant, book-keeper
el experto	expert
ir conociendo	to be getting to know
mostrar (ue)	to show
dar una vuelta	to walk around
la mesa	table
el servicio	toilet
el papel de escribir	writing paper
el sobre	envelope
el armario	cupboard
enseñar	to show
la directora	manager (female)
familiarizarse	to familiarize oneself

PRACTICE 2: Becoming familiar with the office

This is another chance to brush up on and practise office terminology. You should find it quite an easy section as you will be familiar with what it contains. When you have listened a few times, repeat in the pauses trying to reproduce not just the correct pronunciation of each single word but the rhythm and stress of each sentence.

LANGUAGE NOTES

3 **en tal situación**   *in such a situation*
Notice that **tal** means *such a*.

28 **No sé si me voy a acordar de tantas cosas**   *I don't know if I'm going to remember so many things*
Remember that **tanto** and **tanta** mean *so much;* **tantos** and **tantas** *so many*.
tanto dinero *so much money*   **tanta fruta** *so much fruit*
tantos papeles *so many papers* **tantas cartas** *so many letters*

32 **Conocerá a todo el mundo**   *You'll know everybody*
33 **Sabrá dónde está cada uno**   *You'll know where everyone is*
Remember the difference between the two Spanish verbs which mean *to know*, **conocer** and **saber**.

WORDLIST

tal	such a
guardarse	to be kept
abrir	to open
clasificar	to classify, sort
la correspondencia	correspondence
archivar	to file
la factura	bill, invoice
por ejemplo	for example
acordar (ue) de	to remember
tantos	so many

SCENE 3: Rome – In Signor Rossi's office

The story now moves to Rome. Julio is explaining to Signor Rossi, his Italian host, the difficulties he had to get there. Signor Rossi's secretary went to the airport to meet him, but they never met. Rome airport is always so busy ... Julio expresses concern because the secretary may still be looking for him at the airport. Julio wants to know whether he can speak in Spanish at the meeting he is attending in the afternoon. He would also like to be shown round the factory. Signor Rossi is most accommodating.

LANGUAGE NOTES

3   **pero no la encontré**   *but I couldn't find her*
Remember that **poder** is usually left out when what you can not do is an established fact.

7   **cuando se canse de esperar**   *when she gets tired of waiting*
Note that when conjunctions of time like **cuando** or **en cuanto** *as soon as* refer to a future occurrence the verb which comes after them is in the subjunctive.

15   **La culpa es mía**   *It's my fault*
Notice how to apportion blame: **la culpa es tuya.**

16   **¿Podríamos hacer algo ...?**   *Could we do something ...?*
Remember the conditional forms of **poder** (Appendix J).

17   **me preocupa que aún me esté esperando**   *it bothers me that she is still waiting for me*
Note the subjunctive after **me preocupa que.**

WORDLIST

cansarse de	to get tired of
perderse (ie)	to get lost
la entrada	entrance, way in
aparecer	to appear
conocerse	to know each other
preocupar	to worry
la próxima	next time
con claridad	clearly
las instalaciones	installations
el proyector	projector
exactamente	exactly
a largo plazo	long term
poner al corriente	to bring up to date

PRACTICE 3: Arranging to meet somewhere

Making arrangements to meet someone is certainly something you don't want to get wrong and this section gives you a chance to practise some useful terms to use in this respect. When you have listened to the dialogue a few times and can follow it easily, play it through again and in the pauses take the part of the man.

LANGUAGE NOTES

7 **Estación de Chamartín**   *Chamartín Station*
This is one of Madrid's major railway stations.

8 **¿Hay un lugar donde podamos vernos?**   *Is there a place where we could meet?*
The subjunctive is used here after **donde** because the place is vague. It is anywhere suitable for meeting.

10 **Vale**   *O.K.*
You will hear **vale** used countless times in the day to show that something is acceptable to the speaker.

13 **Soy yo Pepe**   *It's (me) Pepe*
The normal way of stating who is speaking on the phone is to use **soy yo** or just **soy.** Similarly if you ask who it is on the other end you use **¿eres tú (Pepe)?**

33 **En el centro mismo de la estación**   *Right in the centre of the station/In the very centre of the station*
35 **me esperas en el mismo sitio**   *wait for me in the same place*
Remember the various meanings of **mismo.**

WORDLIST

ponerse de acuerdo	to arrange, agree
el reloj	clock
la salida	exit, way out
el centro mismo	very centre
hasta el miércoles	see you Wednesday
vamos a ver	let's see

SCENE 4: Rome – in a meeting room

Julio is addressing a group of executives and technicians at the Italian firm he is visiting. He is speaking Spanish in a rather slow and deliberate manner to make himself understood. On the recording you hear extracts from his talk. He tells them about the monthly meetings he is arranging and attempts to classify into four categories the work they are doing in Paris. After the talk and a short break Signor Rossi offers to take Julio out during the evening to see some of Rome's nightspots.

LANGUAGE NOTES

2 **se me ha dicho** *I've been told*
A very useful phrase. Note too **se me dice** *I'm told*.

7 **a principios de este mes** *at the beginning of this month*
Remember **a finales de** *at the end of?*

11 **Cada cuatro semanas** *Every four weeks*
You should note that **cada** *every, each* never changes in form: **cada coche** *every car,* **cada casa** *each house.*

30 **pues no vendría mal** *well I wouldn't mind*
A nice colloquial phrase to use when offered something.

36 **Esta es la mayor** *This is the biggest one*
Note that **mayor** *bigger, biggest* does not change when it describes a feminine noun.

WORDLIST

a principios de	at the beginning of
recoger	to form
el fin	aim, goal
tener lugar	to take place
la categoría	category
el material rodante	rolling stock
el motor	engine
la locomoción	locomotion
el vehículo	vehicle
comprender	to comprise
el tendido de vías	track laying
la construcción	construction, building
la carretera	road, highway
la señalización	sign posting
la programación	programming
el avance	advance
definido	defined
reciente	recent
el terreno	field, domain
sírvase usted mismo	serve yourself
la fábrica	factory
el taller de máquinas	machine shop
principalmente	principally, mostly
pesado	heavy
la línea de montaje	assembly line
la estación de ferrocarril	railway station
no me parece mal	that's not a bad idea
de noche	at night, by night
la vida	life
por aquí	this way
sígame	follow me

PRACTICE 4: An invitation to go out

You should have no difficulty in understanding this section. It deals with some very useful social language about asking someone out. When you have listened to it a few times we want you to do some repeating and role playing. Firstly repeat in the pauses the three basic questions ¿**Vamos a ...?** ¿**Quiere ...?** and ¿**Le gustaría ...?** Then in the pauses in the dialogue take the part of the next speaker.

LANGUAGE NOTES

4 **Practiquémoslas un poco**   *Let's practise them a little*
Notice how the **c** of **practicar** has changed to **qu.**
This always happens to verbs ending in **car** when the verb ending begins with **e.**

6 ¿**Vamos a ...?**   *Shall we go ...?/Let's go ...*
7 ¿**Quiere ...?**   *Do you want ...?*

8 ¿**Le gustaría ...?**   *Would you like ...?*
These are the three basic formulae to which you attach the details of the invitation: ¿**Vamos al cine?** ¿**Quiere tomar algo?** ¿**Le gustaría salir a cenar?** If you are on **tú** terms with someone you would of course use ¿**quieres?** and ¿**te gustaría?**

28 **A mí también me gustaría tomar algo**   *I'd like to have something too*
Remember that **a mí** gives some emphasis to the sentence. In English we do it by stressing *I.*

WORDLIST

igual que	just as
formular	to make up, formulate
libre	free
me encantaría	I'd love to

SCENE 5: In the offices in Paris

Julio is back in Paris. When he arrives at the office he
meets Linda. He hardly remembers her. They greet each
other. Julio wants to know how Linda is doing in her new job
and Linda reciprocates by showing an interest in Julio's trip to
Rome. Next Julio goes to see Luisa in her office. They talk
about the visit to Rome. Julio has come back with a very good
impression of the Italian company. The monthly committee
meetings have finally been arranged. Julio gives Luisa all the
details. Then there is a knock on the door and Linda comes in
with a message.

LANGUAGE NOTES

3   **¿No se acuerda?**   *Don't you remember?*
4   **Me alegro de verte**   *I'm pleased to see you*
As a foreigner and a subordinate in the office Linda uses
usted to Julio while he addresses her as **tú.**

8   **¿Te vas acostumbrando al trabajo?**   *Are you getting
used to the job?*
You can use **ir** and a gerund to indicate a continuous
process as we've already seen with **los iré conociendo** *I'll
be getting to know them.*

26   **¿Buen viaje?**   *Good trip?*
This is the Spanish equivalent to *bon voyage, have a good
trip.* Remember **bueno** drops the **o** before a masculine
noun.

34   **una de las mejores**   *one of the best ones*
Like **mayor, mejor** does not change in the feminine form.

WORDLIST

de verdad	real
serio	serious
hoy por la mañana	this morning
buen viaje	good trip
listo	ready
el mes que viene	next month
se ha acordado	has been agreed
lo del comité de enlace	that business concerning the liaison committee
el tema	topic, subject
debatir	to debate
el pronóstico	forecast
la viabilidad	viability
la evaluación	evaluation
centralizado	centralized
de impresión	very impressive
interrumpir	to interrupt
debería de	you should, ought to

PRACTICE 5: Chatting with someone who is coming back from a trip

Here we return to the topic of talking about how a trip went. You'll hear some of the most useful questions to use if you want to ask someone about a trip and how to answer them. When you have listened a few times play it through again and in the pauses take the part of the following speaker.

LANGUAGE NOTES

1 **¿Quién habrá enviado el télex?** *Who will/might have sent the telex?*
The combination of the future of **haber** and a past participle gives us the future perfect.

4 **al hablar con amigos que han estado fuera** *when talking to friends who have been away*
5 **Si uno ha estado de viaje, al volver se le suele preguntar** *If someone has been on a trip, on his return one usually asks him*
Remember the use of **al** and an infinitive with the meaning *on* or *when*. Remember too that **fuera** can mean *out* or *outside* as well as *away*.

9 **Y si acaba de regresar** *And if he has just returned*
You'll recall that **acabar de** and an infinitive has the sense of *to have just*.

19 **Un poco cansada. El viajar cansa.** *A little tired. Travelling makes you tired.*
20 **Sí que cansa.** *Yes it does (make you tired).*
Note **el viajar** *travelling*. You can add **el** to most infinitives in this way. **Sí que** plus the verb is a good way of expressing agreement.

WORDLIST

habrá enviado	will have sent
estar de viaje	to be on a trip
el viajar	travelling
cansar	to make tired

SCENE 6: In the offices in Paris

This scene follows on from the previous one. Linda has come in with a telex. It is from a high government official in Colombia inviting them to bid for a contract. He is arriving the follwing day and Luisa and her colleagues plan to go and see him at his hotel. Luisa knows the man and thinks they will get the contract. The phone rings. It is M. Leconte for Luisa. The conversation is not very friendly and ends rather abruptly. Linda goes off to get on with her work, while Luisa reminds Julio of an earlier invitation to dinner. She is free tonight. A contract in the offing, dinner with Luisa ... things are looking up.

LANGUAGE NOTES

5   **Del gobierno colombiano**   *From the Colombian government*
Listen carefully to the pronunciation of **Colombia** and **colombiano.**

41   **deberíamos irnos**   *we ought to leave*
Remember that the conditional of **deber** means *should, ought to.*

43   **será mejor que no vuelvas a llamarme**   *it'll be better if you don't ring me again*
Volver a conveys the sense of doing something again.

50   **siento que hayas tenido**   *I'm sorry you've had*
The subjunctive is used because **sentir** *to feel sorry* expresses emotion, just like **esperar** *to hope.*

WORDLIST

colombiano	Colombian
construir	to build, construct
los medios	means
completo	complete
la planificación	planning
la población	population
en un principio	for a start
la previsión	forecast
más de	more than (with a number)
el director general	director general
de hoy a mañana	until tomorrow
el preparativo	preparation
inmejorable	unsurpassable
el servicio de mantenimiento	back-up service
garantizar	to guarantee
la fecha de entrega	delivery date
nuestro	ours
cansar	to bore
la riña	quarrel
durar	to last
la ruptura	break
disgustar	to upset
el disgusto	annoyance
mejorar	to improve

Cassette 4   Side 1
The job in Caracas

SCENE 1: In the offices in Paris

This is a fairly long scene. Jaime, Pablo and Luisa are in
the office discussing the arrangements for the following
day when they are going to meet the Colombian
government's representative. Luisa leaves the room and
the conversation continues between Pablo and Jaime. The
Colombian job is being offered for public bidding. Pablo,
who knows the world of marketing very well, explains
how very often public bidding is rigged so as to produce a
wanted result. Julio comes in and joins the conversation.
They go over the same ground. Pablo expands his theory
on the public bidding system. It does not sound very fair,
but, provided it works in their favour, it does not seem to
worry them. Luisa returns and hears the story from Julio.
The two of them talk about the arrangements for the
evening. They are having dinner together. When Luisa
goes Julio has to put up with a certain amount of leg-
pulling from Pablo and Jaime.

LANGUAGE NOTES

16 **basta con que creemos**   *it's enough for us to create*
Creemos here is not part of **creer** *to think* but the present
subjunctive of **crear** *to create* used after **basta con que.**

38 **No seas inocente**   *Don't be innocent*
Note **seas,** part of the subjunctive of **ser** (App. L).

38 **Se pone un anuncio**   *And ad is placed/One places an
ad/You place an ad/They place an ad*
Notice the different ways of translating this. **Se** is used in
this manner in general impersonal discussions like this and
in the language of the ads themselves. You'll see several
examples in this scene so try to remember how they might
be translated.

45 **Siempre habrá alguno que lo haga**   *There'll always be
somebody who does it*

82 **Tenemos que hacer que elija**   *We must see that he chooses*
Note the subjunctives **haga** from **hacer** and **elija** from **elegir**.

WORDLIST

la noticia	piece of news
a buena hora	in good time
hasta luego	see you later
pronto	soon
bastar con que	to be enough to
crear	to create
salir a	to go out to
la subasta pública	public request for bids
la proposición	proposal
el japonés	Japanese
el sueco	Swede
todo el mundo	everybody
la más barata	the cheapest
de acuerdo con	in accordance with
la ley	law
la mayoría	majority, most
el modo	way, means
sortear	to get round, avoid
inocente	innocent
sacar a concurso	to open to competition
el desarrollo	development
conceder	to grant
el plazo	time limit, interval
detallado	detailed
el cierre	closing, end
astuto	astute, clever, smart
sucio	dirty
era de suponer	I might have guessed
de antemano	beforehand, in advance
la propuesta	proposal
la contabilidad	accountancy
abundar	to abound
lo más probable	the most likely thing
repasar	to check, review
el concurso	competition

la astucia	cunning, astuteness
subastador	opening for bids
la cifra	figure
cuando quieras	whenever you like
con que sí	so then
tener celos	to be jealous
el consuelo	consolation
la camisa	shirt
limpio	clean
afeitado	clean shaven
la colonia	cologne

PRACTICE 1: How to win a contract

Here you have the opportunity to practise some of the business terminology introduced in the previous scene. As usual, listen carefully a few times and then when you are ready take the part in the pauses of the second speaker.

LANGUAGE NOTES

8 **La presentación de proposiciones se cierra el día 30**
The presentation of proposals closes on the 30th
Notice the difference between **cerrar** and **cerrarse** from these examples:
Juan cierra la tienda   *Juan closes the shop*
La tienda se cierra a la una   *The shop closes at one*
The same applies to **abrir** and **abrirse**.
María abrió la puerta   *María opened the door*
La puerta se abrió   *The door opened*

WORDLIST

el hangar	hangar
cerrarse (ie)	to close
de hoy	today's
concurrir	to compete
concursar	to compete

SCENE 2: Paris – in a restaurant

Julio has taken Luisa to a Spanish restaurant in Paris.
They both like it. Julio would like to dance but there is no
dancing tonight. They take some time to choose from the
menu. They discuss various dishes and, eventually, order
their meal. Luisa's order is fairly straightforward, but
Julio is concerned with the size of the portions. He is very
hungry. Not all the dishes on the menu are available. The
waiter recommends some specialities.

LANGUAGE NOTES

20 **Dénos un poco más de tiempo**   *Give us a little more
time*
Dé is the **usted** command form, and present subjunctive,
of **dar** (Appendix L).

22 **Cuando ustedes gusten**   *Whenever you please*
As it is not exactly sure when they will be ready to order
the verb following **cuando** is a subjunctive. In the first
scene we had **cuando quieras** *whenever you like*.

26 **¿cómo es?**   *what's it like?*
This is the usual way of enquiring about the general nature
of both a person or a thing. **¿Cómo es?** *What's he like?*
¿Cómo está? *How is he?* (health)

34 **Yo tengo hambre**   *I'm hungry*
49 **Porque yo tengo mucha hambre**   *Because I'm very
hungry*
Tener hambre is one of a number of idioms involving **tener**
and a noun like **tener fama** *to be famous*, **tener suerte** *to
be lucky*. Look out for more of them.

WORDLIST

¿qué te parece ...?	what do you think of ...?
alguna vez	any time, some time
tener fama	to be famous
el aspecto	appearance
bailar	to dance
el cabaré	cabaret
la nota	sign
la comida	food
la carta	menu
la prisa	hurry
la sopa de espárragos	asparagus soup
la merluza a la romana	hake Roman style
¿cómo es?	what's it like?
rebozado	covered in batter
frito	fried
la caza	game
el faisán	pheasant
la liebre	hare
la página	page
tener hambre	to be hungry
tiene poco que comer	there's little to eat on it
¿qué les pasa?	what's the matter with them?
cocinar	to cook
tómate	have
el plato	dish
la ración	portion
abundante	generous, large
quedar con hambre	to be hungry
la temporada	season
el salmón al horno	baked salmon
la chuletita de cordero	little lamb chop
sabroso	tasty, delicious

PRACTICE 2: What one says in a restaurant

Eating out in a Spanish restaurant can be a considerable
pleasure and this section is devoted to giving you the
chance to practise some of the most useful expressions to
use when choosing and ordering your meal and paying the
bill. When you have listened often enough to be
thoroughly at home with what is said, take the part of the
woman in the pauses on the recording and you'll soon find
how easy it is to deal with the waiter.

LANGUAGE NOTES

2 **se lo piden al camarero**   *they ask the waiter for it*
13 **se la traigo**   *I'll bring it for you*
Note that **se** here does not mean *one* or *self*. It stands for **le**
which always becomes **se** when it precedes **lo, la, le, los,
las** or **les**. In the first sentence the meaning is *to him*, i.e.
to the waiter although we don't translate it here. In second
it means *for you*. Remember that when two third person
object pronouns come together the indirect one (**le** or **les**)
always comes before the direct one and changes to **se.**

16 **sopa de pescado**   *fish soup*
Spanish has two words for *fish:* **pescado** is used for the fish
you buy to eat and **el pez** for a fish which is still alive.

28 **media botella de vino blanco**   *half a bottle of white wine*
Remember not to use **un** or **una** with **medio/a.**

39 **quédese con la vuelta**   *keep the change*
A nice phrase to be able to use to waiters, taxi drivers,
hotel staff etc – provided you back it up with some money!

WORDLIST

lo mismo	the same thing
la lista de vinos	wine list
el escalope de ternera	escalope of veal
la patata	potato
el pescado	fish
de primer plato	as an appetizer
detrás	then, next
la ensalada	salad
la lechuga	lettuce
el tomate	tomato
beber	to drink
la botella	bottle
la cuenta	bill
si hace el favor	if you please
el IVA	Value-Added Tax
el quince por ciento	fifteen percent
quédese con la vuelta	keep the change
la vuelta	change
acompañar a casa	to see someone home

SCENE 3: Paris – in Julio's car

The evening is drawing to a close. Luisa and Julio are saying good night to each other. Julio wants to prolong the occasion. Why not have another drink? Luisa is not so keen. No, not even the proverbial cup of coffee. Julio is insistent but ... Good night and thank you.

LANGUAGE NOTES

4 **el bar al que me llevaste tenía mucho ambiente** *the bar which you took me to had a lot of atmosphere*
This sentence illustrates perfectly one of the differences between the preterite (**llevaste**) and the imperfect (**tenía**). The preterite refers to a single completed action in the past, the imperfect to a more continuous state of affairs: **hacía sol cuando salí** *it was sunny when I left*. Watch out for some irregular preterites in this scene like **estuvo** *was* (4) and **pudiste** *you could* (12).

11 **Como quieras** *As you like*
31 **No es que no quiera** *It's not that I don't want to*
Two useful expressions with the subjunctive of **querer**.

32 **¿Qué te parece si salimos ...?** *How about going out ...?*
¿Qué te parece si ...? is a useful formula to use if you want to ask someone's opinion of your suggestion.

WORDLIST

dar las gracias por	to thank for
la velada	evening out
tomar una copa	to have a drink
retirarse	to go off to bed
con hambre	hungry
el bocadillo	snack
invitar a entrar	to invite in
¿qué tiene de malo?	what's wrong with that?
insistir	to insist
mañana por la noche	tomorrow night

PRACTICE 3: Farewells

We focus here on thanking someone for a night out and saying good night. It is based on the scene between Luisa and Julio after their evening at the restaurant. This is another section where we would like you to role play rather than repeat. Listen a few times and then in the pauses take the part of the next speaker, following the cues given – they are in brackets in the book.

LANGUAGE NOTES

1 **¿Qué dice ella?**   *What does she say?*

2 **El no está de acuerdo**   *He doesn't agree*
As you know the subject pronouns are not used very often. Here, however, it is essential to use **él** and **ella** to avoid any confusion.

2 **Es hora de**   *It's time to*
Note that **hora** is used in this fixed expression: **es hora de levantarse** *it's time to get up,* **es hora de salir** *it's time to leave.*

4 **fue una velada muy agradable**   *it was a very pleasant evening*
5 **estuvo muy bien**   *it was fine*
Although the evening out lasted a few hours it is now over and can be looked on as a completed event: hence the use of the preterite tense **(fue** and **estuvo).**

13 **Que descanses**   *Sleep well*
Literally this says *may you rest.*

15 **en el hotel donde se hospeda**   *in the hotel where he's staying*
Hospedarse is used for *to stay* in relation to hotels etc.

WORDLIST

la despedida	farewell
al día siguiente	on the following day
encantado	delighted
que descanses	sleep well
a la mañana siguiente	on the following morning
hospedarse	to stay, put up

SCENE 4: In the offices in Paris and in Sr. Cortés's hotel

The morning after Julio arrives at the office. Pablo wants to know how he got on the night before. Then Luisa arrives and all four leave to go and meet Sr. Cortés. The scene switches to Sr. Cortés's hotel. Luisa tálks to one of the receptionists. She wants her to contact Sr. Cortés in his room. Presently Sr. Cortés – whose first name is Pedro – comes down and meets Luisa and her team.

LANGUAGE NOTES

7 **Quiero decir que si lo pasaste bien anoche**   *I mean did you have a good time last night*
Here Pablo is explaining what he meant when he asked Julio **¿Qué tal?** Julio obviously thought he had asked him how he was rather than how the night had gone.

38 **Tan guapa como siempre**   *As beautiful as ever*
Remember **tan … como** *as … as* and **más … que** *more … than* (**tan guapa como siempre; más guapa que siempre**).

44 **¿Cuánto hace que no nos vemos?**   *How long is it since we've seen each other?*

45 **Debe de hacer cinco años**   *It must be five years*
Notice how **hacer** is used in these expressions of time and that the verb used (**nos vemos**) is in the present tense. **Deber de** indicates supposition on the speaker's part.

53 **Oye, vamos a tutearnos**   *Listen, let's call each other tú*
An informal way of making this suggestion.

WORDLIST

contar (ue)	to tell
¿y qué?	so? so what?
meterse	to interfere, meddle
allá tú	up to you
el salón	lounge
en ti no se nota	it doesn't show on you
¿cuánto hace que ...?	how long is it since ...

PRACTICE 4: Meeting acquaintances

More practice here on the social pleasantries, this time
concerning what to say when you meet acquaintances you
have not seen for some time. When you have listened a
few times to catch the general meaning, you should play
through the recording again paying attention to the cue
sentences that the man utters. These indicate the kind of
thing the next speaker is going to say. Link the two in your
mind so that you can then play through once more and in
the pauses take the part of the following speaker.

LANGUAGE NOTES

1 **se conocen desde hace unos años**   *they've known each
other for some years*
In the previous scene you saw how **hace** and the present
tense are used in these expressions of time. Notice that
desde is often inserted before **hace**. The question
¿cuánto tiempo hace? can also be expressed as **¿desde hace
cuánto tiempo?**

9 **La conocí en Valencia**   *I met her in Valencia*
31 **Nos conocimos en Valencia**   *We met in Valencia*
Remember **conocer** and **conocerse** can also mean *to meet.*

9 **Hace cinco o seis años**   *Five or six years ago*
Don't forget that **hace** also means *ago.*

32 **Sí que lo recuerdo**   *Yes I do remember*
Once again **sí que** adds emphasis to the remark.

42 **Y no hemos vuelto a vernos desde entonces**   *And we
haven't seen each other again since then*
Remember **volver a** meaning *to do again?*

WORDLIST

desde hace unos años	for some years
saludarse	to greet each other
inesperadamente	unexpectedly
reconocer	to recognize
responder	to reply
sorprenderse	to be surprised
tanto tiempo	so long
las negociaciones	negotiations
el encuentro	meeting
el conocido	acquaintance

SCENE 5: In Sr. Cortés' hotel

Pablo is explaining to Sr. Cortés the advantages and disadvantages of various transport systems. He points out that their company is in a position to set up any of them fairly promptly and at a very competitive price. They discuss dates for the submission of bids. Luisa feels they need to have more information made available to them. And then the conversation takes on a different tone. Luisa wants to know their chances of getting the contract. Sr. Cortés is in a delicate position and can only give an off-the-record answer.

LANGUAGE NOTES

4 **no disponemos de él**   *we don't have it*
Remember **disponer de** *to have (available)*, relating to things like time or money or, as here, space.

26 **no hay quien los mejore**   *there's nobody who can top them*

28 **A los que nos ofrezcan**   *those who offer us*
The subjunctives are used here after a negative antecedent **no hay quien** and an indefinite one where Pablo is referring to any supplier who can offer the best deal.

58 **Hombre, no puedo decíroslo**   *Look, I can't tell you that*
Hombre can be used just as an exclamation.

61 **antes de ver**   *before seeing*
Don't forget to insert **de** between **antes** and an infinitive.

71 **Hay que esperar**   *You must wait*

WORDLIST

el resultado	result
el espacio	space
evitar	to avoid
cometido	committed
planear	to plan
lo último	the latest thing
rápido	fast, quick
el rendimiento	performance, efficiency
el consumo energético	energy consumption
bajo	low
contar con	to have
proponer	to propose, present
desplazarse	to travel
en principio	in principle
seleccionar	to choose, select
el proveedor	supplier
el beneficio	benefit
la pregunta clave	key question
entregar	to deliver, hand in
esbozado	outlined
el presupuesto	budget
cuanto más reducido mejor	the lower the better
sería lo ideal	that would be the ideal
el carburante	fuel
el gasoil	diesel oil
la mano de obra	workforce
con franqueza	frankly
el gasto	cost, expense
reembolsar	to reimburse
algo es algo	it's better than nothing

PRACTICE 5: Making plans

This section not surprisingly deals with the language used in bidding for a contract. As with recent practice sections, take the part of the second speaker in the pauses after you have listened to the recording a number of times.

LANGUAGE NOTES

5 **¿Para cuándo?**   *By when?*
Note that in expressions of future time like this **para** can mean *by*. Remember **para finales de año** *by the end of the year* in the previous scene?

11 **Necesitamos más de seis semanas**   *We need more than six weeks*
Remember **más de** instead of **más que** before a number.

17 **¿Cuánto tiempo llevaría fabricarlo?**   *How long would it take to make it?*
You've seen **llevar** used in this time sense before. Note that **fabricar** means *to make* in the sense of *to manufacture*.

27 **no podemos garantizar que esté listo**   *we can't guarantee that it'll be ready*
Note the subjunctive (**esté**) here after **no podemos garantizar.**

33 **Pero que no pase de ocho semanas**   *But don't let it be longer than eight weeks*
A useful type of expression to use to lay down a time limit.

35 **Haré lo que pueda**   *I'll do whatever I can*
You'll remember that we use the subjunctive after **lo que.**

WORDLIST

fijar plazos	to fix dates
el prototipo	prototype
¿para cuándo?	by when?
fabricar	to make, manufacture
probar (ue)	to test
transportar	to transport
el plazo	time limit
prudente	wise, prudent
es de suponer	it is to be supposed
optimista	optimistic

SCENE 6: Paris – in Luisa's car and in the offices

Luisa and Julio are driving back to the office. They both
have a very favourable impression of their meeting with
Sr. Cortés. In the optimistic atmosphere Julio invites
Luisa to go out in the evening, but she sees little point in
it. After all, Julio will soon be off to South America and
that will be the end of the relationship. They arrive at the
office. Pablo is already there. He is also feeling optimistic
about getting the Colombian contract. Julio and Luisa
continue their private conversation. Pablo does not
understand what is going on between them. The phone
rings. It is M. Leconte who wants to speak to Luisa. Luisa
has the call transferred to her own office. Suddenly Julio
makes up his mind about the Caracas job and tells Pablo
about it. Luisa returns to resume her conversation with
Julio, but he feels there is nothing else to say. His mind is
made up, it appears.

LANGUAGE NOTES

4   **Y no lo sabremos hasta finales del verano**   *And we
won't know until the end of the summer*
Sabremos is part of the future tense of **saber** (App. E).

46   **¿te importaría pasar esta llamada a mi despacio?**
would you mind putting this call through to my office?

48   **Voy a conectarle. Ya puede hablar.**   *I'll put you
through. You're through now.*
Some very useful telephone language in the above
sentences which is well worth noting.

WORDLIST

el verano	summer
la decisión	decision
por	because of
conducir	to lead
magnífico	great, magnificent
extraordinario	outstanding
conectar	to connect
acabarse	to be over
tener razón	to be right
no pintar nada	to cut no ice
diferente	different
sacar de quicio	to irritate
manos a la obra	let's get to work
se ve que	it can be seen that
el optimismo	optimism
compartir	to share

Cassette 4 Side 2
Julio is going away

SCENE 1: In the offices in Paris

In this scene Julio is dictating some letters to the secretary. The first letter is addresse_ to someone in Caracas. It appears that Julio has changed his mind about going to Venezuela once again. In fact he changes his mind about the letter itself! He starts dictating a second letter. This one is for a colleague in Madrid explaining his change of mind and requesting his support. After all, he wants to stay in Paris.

LANGUAGE NOTES

3 **Distinguido señor Alvarez de la Vega**   *Dear Sr. Alvarez de la Vega*
5 **Doy respuesta a su escrito del pasado día ...**   *In reply to your letter of ...*
This is an example of how to start a formal letter, with **distinguido** an alternative to **estimado.**

19 **Necesito que alguien me ayude**   *I need someone to help me*
The subjunctive is used after **alguien** here because it is indefinite. Julio doesn't mind who it is as long as someone does help. It is an indefinite antecedent.

24 **Sí tú necesitases**   *If you needed/were to need*
Necesitases is an imperfect subjunctive. We'll look at this usage later on.

WORDLIST

la fecha de hoy	today's date
distinguido señor	dear sir
dos puntos	colon
dar respuesta	to reply
el escrito	letter
plantear	to put to
el asunto	matter, subject
delicado	delicate
cambiar de parecer	to change one's mind
justificar	to justify
el cambio de parecer	change of mind
preguntarse	to wonder
ya está	that's it
la fecha de ayer	yesterday's date

PRACTICE 1: Correspondence

Now some guidance on letter writing in Spanish of both formal and informal character. The female speaker asks the male about various aspects of letter writing and he supplies the necessary information. You will notice that Spanish is rather more flowery in the terms it uses for letters than English. Listen as usual and then in the pauses take the man's part.

LANGUAGE NOTES

2 **Para ello ha enviado una carta**   *For that reason he has sent a letter*

Literally **ello** means *it* but it doesn't refer to a specific thing as do **él** and **ella.** Here it refers to everything involved in Julio's changing his mind. It is similar in this respect to other vague, indefinite words like **esto, eso, lo que** etc.

7 **¿qué se pone en la parte de arriba a la derecha?**   *what does one put at the top on the right side?*

You will find **se** *one* used throughout this section as the information is sought and given in an impersonal manner. **Arriba** means *up, above* and in line 11 you'll see its opposite **abajo** *down below.*

28 **Dos puntos**   *A colon*

In a Spanish letter you put a colon and not a comma at the beginning of the letter; **Querido Julio:** *Dear Julio,*

36 **No se puede decir que presente muchas dificultades**
    One can't say that it presents many difficulties

The subjunctive is used after **no se puede decir que.**

WORDLIST

para ello	for that reason
componer	to compose
en la parte de arriba	at the top
abajo	down, below
el encabezamiento	heading
la referencia	reference
ambos	both
muy señor(es) mío(s)	dear sir(s)
íntimo	close
despedirse (i)	to sign off
la carta de negocios	business letter
recibe un cordial saludo	regards, with best wishes
concluir	to conclude, finish
la firma	signature

SCENE 2: In the offices in Paris

Julio arrives at the office and is told by Linda, the
secretary, that there is a problem with the forthcoming
committee meeting. There has been a phone call from
Rome. The Italian representative cannot come on the
agreed date. Julio is unwilling to accept this and tells
Linda to phone back, to speak to the right person, and to
impress upon him the need to attend.

LANGUAGE NOTES

11 **¿Quién ha dicho eso?**   *Who has said that?*
27 **Esto es lo que tienes que hacer**   *This is what you must do*
      Esto refers not to a specific object but to everything said.
      Similarly **esto** refers to everything that is to be done.

13 **ya habíamos acordado la fecha**   *we'd already agreed the*
      date
15 **Pero dijo que no podía**   *But he said he couldn't*
      There is a mixture of past tenses used in this scene. Look
      out for them and check in the Appendix (F,H,I) if necessary.

17 **¿A qué viene entonces?**   *What's he coming for then?*
      Note the question **¿a qué viene?** *what's he/she coming for?*

32 **Como usted diga**   *As you say*
      Another fixed expression using the subjunctive.

33 **Y si tienes problema alguno**   *And if you have any*
      problem at all
      Placing **alguno** after **problema** makes it more emphatic.

WORDLIST

nadie más	nobody else
como usted diga	just as you say

PRACTICE 2: Instructions and orders

This section is all about giving instructions and orders. It takes the form of a dialogue in an office where a slight mishap has occurred and where instructions are issued in both **tú** and **usted** forms. Listen carefully to grasp the general meaning and when you are ready play through the recording again speaking in the pauses the instructions the woman gives to her colleague – in other words playing her part.

LANGUAGE NOTES

1 **La gente de Roma le está creando muchos problemas a Julio**
The people from Rome are creating many problems for Julio
Note **de Roma** means from Rome on this occasion, as we are not talking about all the people of Rome, just Julio's colleagues there. Note too **a Julio** *for Julio.*

7 **se ha enganchado la corbata**   *has caught his tie*
In Spanish it is usual to use just the definite article with clothes and parts of the body rather than the possessive (**mi, tu, su** etc.). At the same time ownership is often indicated by the use of the reflexive pronoun as here. Another example: **me he enganchado la corbata** *I've caught my tie.*

14 **Dígale que se calme**   *Tell him to keep calm*
15 **¡Cálmate!**   *Keep calm*
28 **No lo dejes caer**   *Don't drop it*
As you see the man addresses the woman as **usted,** while she addresses her colleague as **tú.** You can refresh your memory about these command forms by looking again at Appendix C. Remember that all except the positive **tú** (and **vosotros**) commands are part of the present subjunctive and that in the negative commands pronouns precede the verb.

WORDLIST

enfadarse	to get angry
la orden	order
dar órdenes	to give orders
utilizarse	to be used
el compañero	companion, colleague
enganchar	to catch
la corbata	tie
la multicopista	copy machine
calmarse	to keep calm
tirar de	to pull, tug
apagar	to turn off
la tapa	cover
pulsar	to press
levantar	to lift
el rodillo	roller
superior	top, upper
dejar caer	to drop
hacer girar	to turn, spin
bajar	to lower
conectar	to switch on, plug in
basta de	enough

SCENE 3: In the offices in Paris

Linda comes into Julio's office to let him know that her
phone call to Rome has done the trick. Julio congratulates
her. Then the conversation drifts towards Julio's future.
He does not want to leave. Linda urges him to discuss it
with Luisa. Luisa comes in and Linda exits. Julio wants to
know how Luisa's relationship with M. Leconte is developing.
The news is not discouraging for him. Then he asks
whether it would be possible for him to stay in Paris and .
keep his job. Luisa is sympathetic, but unfortunately the
job has already been offered to some other person,
someone Julio knows. When he hears the name he feels
that insult is being added to injury.

LANGUAGE NOTES

7 **pero que vendrá**   *but that he will come*
As you see the future of **venir** is an irregular one.

10 **Tengo entendido**   *I gather*
This is a very useful idiom to have at your command.

12 **No parece que tenga muchas ganas de irse**   *You don't
seem very keen to go*
There'll be more about **tener ganas de** a little later.

18 **Estoy segura de que ella quiere que se quede**   *I'm sure
she wants you to stay*
24 **no es seguro**   *isn't certain/sure*
Note that you use **estar** with **seguro** when people are
giving an opinion and **ser** with **seguro** about things, here
el trabajo.

WORDLIST

mostrarse (ue)	to be, show oneself
duro	tough, hard
tengo entendido	I gather
tener ganas de	to feel like
ser seguro	to be sure (things)
complicar	to complicate
sin necesidad	unnecessarily
existir	to exist
disgustar	to displease
reemplazar	to replace
poner al corriente	to brief
portarse con	to behave towards
echar	to throw out

PRACTICE 3: Listen in order to understand (3)

Here is another of the practice sections where we just want you to listen for meaning. In it a woman reports a phone message she has just received. When she has said her piece a man joins the conversation and they go through the message together, breaking it down into short snippets. Finally you hear the woman repeating what she said earlier. There is very little new vocabulary here, so just sit back and listen as often as you need to, taking in as much as you can.

LANGUAGE NOTES

6 **Es de una tal señora Sánchez**   *It's from a certain Sra. Sánchez*
Remember this use of **tal** which usually means *such*.

11 **oyó decir que el señor Moreno se va al extranjero**   *she heard that Sr. Moreno is going abroad*
Notice the expression **oír decir** which is used in the sense of to have learned about something.
Note also **irse al extranjero** *to go abroad* and **estar en el extranjero** *to be abroad*. The noun **extranjero** means *foreigner:* **soy extranjero/a** *I'm a foreigner.*

WORDLIST

de manera que	so that
el aviso telefónico	phone message
oír decir	to hear (tell)
irse al extranjero	to go abroad
excepto	except
hacerse cargo de	to take over

157

SCENE 4: In the offices in Paris

Luisa introduces Sr. Escudero to Julio. Of course, they
have met before and there is no love lost between them.
Luisa leaves the two men on their own and during the rest
of the scene they discuss the committee meeting they will
be attending in the afternoon, and the reasons why Sr.
Escudero has come to replace Julio in Paris. Julio does not
find Sr. Escudero's arguments very convincing and the
conversation takes on unfriendly tones.

LANGUAGE NOTES

9 **Será mejor que os deje para que habléis**   *It'll be best if
I leave you to talk*
Note the subjunctives here: **deje** after **será mejor que**
and **habléis** after **para que.**

12 **Será mejor olvidar lo pasado**   *It'll be best to forget the
past/what is past*

43 **Lo mejor será que vuelva**   *The best thing is for you to
go back*
Notice here the use of **lo** with an adjective and the different
ways in which it can be translated.

14 **yo voy de espectador**   *I'm going as a spectator*
Note how **de** here has the meaning of *as a.*

42 **Usted no sirve para este trabajo. No es lo suyo.**   *You are
not suitable for this job. It's not for you.*
Remember **es lo tuyo** earlier?
Note too **servir para: no sirve para nada** *it's useless.*

WORDLIST

por cierto	certainly, that's for certain
lo pasado	the past, what's past
el espectador	spectator
hacerse una idea de	to get an idea of
de todos modos	in any case
enterarse de	to understand
en serio	seriously
apropiado	suitable
anterior	previous
servir (i) para	to be suitable for
no es lo suyo	it's not for you
lo mejor	the best thing
quedarse con las ganas	to fail, be disappointed
dudar	to doubt
ocurrir	to happen
hacer el tonto	to play the fool

PRACTICE 4: Feeling like doing something

This section is designed to give you some practice in a very common and useful expression to use when you want to indicate that you feel like doing something. We refer to **tener ganas de** which you have already encountered. Here a man is asking a lady called Mercedes if she would like to do various things. She replies using **ganas** in various ways. Listen a few times to grasp what is going on, then, in the pauses, speak the lady's lines. In the last pause you will be speaking the man's final and ironic line.

LANGUAGE NOTES

9 **No tengo ganas de ir al cine**   *I'm not eager to go to the movies/I don't feel like going to the movies*
The basic idiom is, then, **tener ganas de** followed by the infinitive. As you see you can vary the English translation.

16 **Y yo no tengo ganas de aguantarte**   *And I'm getting fed up with you*
Literally this says *I don't feel like putting up with you.*
We hope you never have to say this in Spanish.

22 **¡Te vas a quedar con las ganas!**   *You're going to be disappointed!*
This is another useful expression with **ganas.**

23 **Julio sigue con ganas de quedarse en París**   *Julio continues to want to stay in Paris*
You can use **ganas** with a number of verbs as you can see with **seguir con ganas de.** Note **esperar con ganas** *to look forward to.*

WORDLIST

el cine	cinema
poner	to show
la película	film
las afueras	suburbs, outskirts
aguantar	to put up with
seguir (i) con ganas	to continue to want

SCENE 5: Paris – in the offices of the holding company

The scene begins with Sr. Escudero and Julio at the committee meeting. Sr. Escudero is rather impressed by what he hears. Julio goes out to make a phone call. Next we hear Julio speaking with Linda on the phone. He wants to know whether there has been any message for him. There is a telex. There is a letter from Caracas too, which Linda reads over the phone. Much to Julio's surprise the letter confirms his Venezuelan appointment, provided he passes a medical. Back at the meeting Julio is wondering how he can fail the medical. He goes out and phones the office again to enquire about the telex. It is from Marisa! It explains a great deal. Julio feels he is reaching the end of his tether.

LANGUAGE NOTES

2 **Son de lo mejor que hay** *They're among the best there are*

29 **Nos gustaría que se incorporase**   *We'd like you to join*
75 **"Les dije que necesitabas una secretaria que te entendiese**
I told them you needed a secretary who understood you
The imperfect subjunctives **incorporase** and **entendiese** are used because they depend on verbs in the conditional tense (**gustaría**) and preterite (**dije**). See Appendix L & M.

49 **Rómpase una pierna**   *Break a leg*
51 **le diga que se quite la ropa**   *tells you to take your clothes off*
The reflexive **se** indicates that it is your own leg and own clothes that are involved and not someone else's!

WORDLIST

leer	to read
entero	all
es muy de mi agrado	I'm very pleased
incorporarse a	to join
lo antes posible	as early as possible
un examen médico	a medical examination
el médico	doctor
puro	pure
el trámite	formality
la enfermedad	illness
lo malo	the bad thing
sano	healthy
doler (ue)	to hurt, have a pain
romperse	to break
la pierna	leg
hágase el sordo	pretend to be deaf
quitarse la ropa	to take off one's clothes
olvidarse de	to forget
privado	private
confidencial	confidential
cariñito mío	my darling
¡qué más da!	what does it matter?
el colchón	mattress
el agua (fem.)	water
valer	to be worth
falta un poco	there's a bit more
tirar	to throw away
el beso	kiss
se acabó	that's the end
el veneno	poison

PRACTICE 5: When one doesn't feel well

Unfortunately you might have to visit a doctor in a Spanish-speaking country and this section gives you practice in some of the key expressions to use and some of the more common ailments. Listen to the recording a few times and then take the part of the patient visiting the doctor in the pauses.

LANGUAGE NOTES

1 **sugiere a Julio que se haga el enfermo**   *suggests to Julio that he pretend to be ill*
Note the expression **hacerse el enfermo.** You might recall the remark **hágase el sordo** *pretend to be deaf* in the previous scene.

6 **No me encuentro bien**   *I don't feel well*
This is an alternative to **no me siento bien.**

8 **Me duele la cabeza**   *I've got a headache*
This is an alternative to **tengo dolor de cabeza. Doler** means *to hurt* and can be used with any part of the body: **me duele la pierna** *my leg hurts*, **me duelen los pies** *my feet are hurting*.

17 **¿Qué tiene usted?**   *What's the trouble?*
This is the question a doctor is likely to use.

31 **Sólo regular. Tengo algo de diarrea.**   *Only so-so. I've got a touch of diarrhea.*
Regular is quite a handy word to know. It doesn't give very much away! Note **tener algo de** *to have a touch of.*

WORDLIST

encontrarse (ue) bien	to be well
sugerir (ie)	to suggest
hacerse el enfermo	to feign illness
me duele la cabeza	I've got a headache
el malestar	discomfort
el estómago	stomach
la indigestión	indigestion
hacer daño	to harm, upset
el síntoma	symptom
¿qué tiene usted?	what's the trouble?
me duele el estómago	I've got a stomachache
fuera de lo normal	out of the ordinary, unusual
excederse	to overdo it
el intestino	intestine, bowel
funcionar	to function
regular	so-so
algo de diarrea	a touch of diarrhea
la medicina	medicine
la comida	meal
con moderación	moderately
el mal	ill
la cura	cure

SCENE 6: Paris – in a travel agency and at the airport

The scene begins at a travel agency where Julio is getting a plane ticket for Caracas. The scene switches to the airport. We hear the anouncement for the flight to Caracas. Luisa and Julio are saying goodbye to each other. There is a certain sadness in their voices. Who knows, in three year's time, after his contract expires, Julio might return to Paris. But, in the meantime, he is off to Caracas where Marisa is awaiting his arrival.

LANGUAGE NOTES

5 **El primer vuelo disponible**   *The first flight available*
Just like **bueno, malo** and **alguno, primero** loses the **o** before a masculine noun. This is known as apocopation.

27 **Cuando termine tu contrato en Caracas ...**   *When your contract in Caracas ends ...*
Remember that the subjunctive is used after **cuando** when the future is referred to.

29 **¿Cuánto dura el contrato?**   *How long does the contract last?*
As you see **cuánto tiempo** can be shortened to **cuánto**.

33 **será mejor que arranques**   *you'd better be off*
In the subjunctive of verbs ending in **-car,** the **c** changes to **qu.** This is because the verb ending begins with **e.**

36 **Y que tengáis suerte con lo de Colombia**   *And good luck with the Colombia business*

165

WORDLIST

directo	direct
perfectamente	perfect
el altavoz	loudspeaker
anunciar	to announce
con destino a	destination
la puerta	gate
un buen día	one fine day
arrancar	to get going
llevar bien	to get along well

APPENDIX

Appendix

A   Verbs – The Present Tense

REGULAR VERBS

-ar: tomar – tomo, tomas, toma, tomamos, tomáis, toman
-er: comer – como, comes, come, comemos, coméis, comen
-ir: vivir –   vivo, vives, vive, vivimos, vivís, viven
The following have a spelling change in the **yo** form but are
otherwise regular: verbs ending in **-cer (pertenecer – pertenezco)**,
in **-ger (coger – cojo)**, in **-gir (dirigir – dirijo)**, in-**ucir (conducir
– conduzco)**.
Verbs ending in **-uir** also have a spelling change as follows:
**contribuir – contribuyo, contribuyes, contribuye, contribuimos,
contribuís, contribuyen.**

IRREGULAR VERBS

dar –   doy, das, da, damos, dais, dan
decir –   digo, dices, dice, decimos, decís, dicen
estar –   estoy, estás, está, estamos, estáis, están
haber –   he, has, ha, hemos, habéis, han
ir –   voy, vas, va, vamos, vais, van
oír –   oigo, oyes, oye, oímos, oís, oyen
ser –   soy, eres, es, somos, sois, son
tener –   tengo, tienes, tiene, tenemos, tenéis, tienen
venir –   vengo, vienes, viene, venimos, venís, vienen
ver –   veo, ves, ve, vemos, veis, ven
The following are irregular in the **yo** form only:
**caer – caigo; hacer – hago; poner – pongo; saber – sé; salir –
salgo; traer – traigo.**

B   Verbs – The Gerund

-ar verbs: **tomar – tomando**
-er/-ir verbs: **comer – comiendo; vivir – viviendo**
Note the following irregular forms: **caer – cayendo; contribuir –
contribuyendo; decir – diciendo; dormir – durmiendo; ir – yendo;
leer – leyendo; oír – oyendo; poder – pudiendo; traer – trayendo;
venir – viniendo.**

C Verbs – The Imperative

Regular verbs	tú	usted	vosotros	ustedes
tomar	toma	tome	tomad	tomen
comer	come	coma	comed	coman
vivir	vive	viva	vivid	vivan

There are no irregular **vosotros** forms but note these irregular
tú forms: **decir – di; hacer – haz; ir – ve; poner – pon; salir
– sal; tener – ten; venir – ven.**
The **usted** and **ustedes** commands and all negative commands
are forms of the present subjunctive:
tomar – no tomes, no tome, no toméis, no tomen
comer – no comas, no coma, no comáis, no coman
vivir –　no vivas, no viva, no viváis, no vivan
Irregular **usted/ustedes** forms are: **dar – dé, den; estar –
esté, estén; ir – vaya, vayan; saber – sepa, sepan; ser – sea, sean.**

D Root changing Verbs

o – ue: poder – puedo, puedes, puede, podemos, podéis, pueden
e – ie: querer – quiero, quieres, quiere, queremos, queréis,
quieren
e – i: pedir – pido, pides, pide, pedimos, pedís, piden
The last group are all **-ir** verbs and also make the change in the
gerund **(pidiendo)**, the third person forms of the preterite **(pidió,
pidieron)** and the **nosotros** form of the present subjunctive
(pidamos). The same applies to **-ir** verbs which change **e** to **ie**,
like **sentir** and **servir (sintiendo; sintió, sintieron; sintamos:
sirviendo; sirvió, sirvieron; sirvamos).** The root change also
takes place in the present subjunctive: **poder – pueda, puedas,**
etc.; **querer – quiera** etc.; **pedir – pida** etc.

E Verbs – The Future Tense

REGULAR VERBS

The endings are added to the infinitive, whether **-ar, -er** or
-ir. Hence:
**tomar – tomaré, tomarás, tomará, tomaremos, tomaréis,
tomarán**
**comer – comeré, comerás, comerá, comeremos, comeréis,
comerán**

IRREGULAR FORMS

The endings are the same as for regular verbs but the stem is different:

decir – diré, dirás, dirá, diremos, diréis, dirán
haber – habré, habrás, habrá, habremos, habréis, habrán
hacer – haré, harás, hará, haremos, haréis, harán
poder – podré, podrás, podrá, podremos, podréis, podrán
poner – pondré, pondrás, pondrá, pondremos, pondréis, pondrán
querer –querré, querrás, querrá, querremos, querréis, querrán
saber – sabré, sabrás, sabrá, sabremos, sabréis, sabrán
salir – saldré, saldrás, saldrá, saldremos, saldréis, saldrán
tener – tendré, tendrás, tendrá, tendremos, tendréis, tendrán
valer – valdré, valdrás, valdrá, valdremos, valdréis, valdrán

The future of **haber** + part participle forms the future perfect: **habré hecho.**

F   Verbs – The Imperfect Tense

REGULAR VERBS

tomar – tomaba, tomabas, tomaba, tomábamos, tomabais,
        tomaban
comer – comía, comías, comía, comíamos, comíais, comían
vivir – vivía, vivías, vivía, vivíamos, vivíais, vivían

There are only three irregular ones, as follows:
ir – iba, ibas, iba, íbamos, ibais, iban
ser – era, eras, era, éramos, erais, eran
ver – veía, veías, veía, veíamos, veíais, veían

G   Verbs – The Perfect Tense

This is formed by the present tense of **haber** and the past participle:
tomar – he tomado, has tomado, ha tomado, hemos tomado,
        habéis tomado, han tomado
comer – he comido etc.   vivir – he vivido etc.
The following verbs have an irregular past participle:
decir – dicho; hacer – hecho; poner – puesto; romper – roto;
ver – visto.

H   Verbs – The Preterite Tense

REGULAR VERBS

tomar – tomé, tomaste, tomó, tomamos, tomasteis, tomaron
comer – comí, comiste, comió, comimos, comisteis, comieron
vivir –   viví, viviste, vivió, vivimos, vivisteis, vivieron

IRREGULAR VERBS

andar –	anduve, anduviste, anduvo, anduvimos, anduvisteis, anduvieron
caer –	caí, caíste, cayó, caímos, caísteis, cayeron
conducir –	conduje, condujiste, condujo, condujimos, condujisteis, condujeron
dar –	di, diste, dio, dimos, disteis, dieron
decir –	dije, dijiste, dijo, dijimos, dijisteis, dijeron
dormir –	dormí, dormiste, durmió, dormimos, dormisteis, durmieron
estar –	estuve, estuviste, estuvo, estuvimos, estuvisteis, estuvieron
haber –	hube, hubiste, hubo, hubimos, hubisteis, hubieron
hacer –	hice, hiciste, hizo, hicimos, hicisteis, hicieron
ir –	fui, fuiste, fue, fuimos, fuisteis, fueron
oír –	oí, oíste, oyó, oímos, oísteis, oyeron
poder –	pude, pudiste, pudo, pudimos, pudisteis, pudieron
poner –	puse, pusiste, puso, pusimos, pusisteis, pusieron
querer –	quise, quisiste, quiso, quisimos, quisisteis, quisieron
saber –	supe, supiste, supo, supimos, supisteis, supieron
ser –	fui, fuiste, fue, fuimos, fuisteis, fueron
tener –	tuve, tuviste, tuvo, tuvimos, tuvisteis, tuvieron
traer –	traje, trajiste, trajo, trajimos, trajisteis, trajeron
venir –	vine, viniste, vino, vinimos, vinisteis, vinieron
ver –	vi, viste, vio, vimos, visteis, vieron

Verbs ending in **-car** and **-gar** insert **u** in the **yo** form:
practicar – **practiqué, practicaste** etc. (Note the **q.**)
pagar –   **pagué, pagaste** etc.

I Verbs – The Pluperfect Tense

This is formed by the imperfect of **haber** and the past participle:
había tomado, habías tomado, había tomado, habíamos tomado, habíais tomado, habían tomado

J Verbs – The Conditional Tense

The endings are added to the infinitive in the case of regular verbs and to the stem used for the future tense in the case of irregular ones (see Appendix E).
tomar – tomaría, tomarías, tomaría, tomaríamos, tomaríais, tomarían
poder – podría, podrías, podría, podríamos, podríais, podrían
The conditional of **haber** and a past participle form the conditional perfect tense:
habría comido, habrías comido etc.

K Reflexive Verbs

These may be of any type (**-ar, -er, -ir**) and may be regular or irregular. They have in common the reflexive pronouns (**me, te, se, nos, os, se**).
irse – me voy, te vas, se va, nos vamos, os vais, se van
The reflexive pronouns come directly before the verb in all tenses: **me levantaré; se ha ido; nos levantábamos.**
With the infinitive and gerund the reflexive pronoun is either attached to the end of the verb or placed before a preceding verb on which the infinitive or gerund depend:
voy a sentarme or **me voy a sentar; está levantándose** or
se está levantando.
The pronouns come on the end of imperatives except when they are negative:
levántate but **no te levantes; vete** but **no te vayas.**

L Verbs – The Subjunctive Forms

PRESENT SUBJUNCTIVE

tomar – **tome, tomes, tome, tomemos, toméis, tomen**
comer – **coma, comas, coma, comamos, comáis, coman**
vivir – **viva, vivas, viva, vivamos, viváis, vivan**
The present subjunctive is formed from the **yo** form of the
present indicative. The only verbs where this does not occur are
those whose **yo** form does not end in **-o.** Hence those formed
regularly are:
caer – **caiga, caigas, caiga, caigamos, caigáis, caigan**
decir – **diga, digas, diga, digamos, digáis, digan**
hacer – **haga, hagas, haga, hagamos, hagáis, hagan**
oír – **oiga, oigas, oiga, oigamos, oigáis, oigan**
poner – **ponga, pongas, ponga, pongamos, pongáis, pongan**
salir – **salga, salgas, salga, salgamos, salgáis, salgan**
tener – **tenga, tengas, tenga, tengamos, tengáis, tengan**
traer – **traiga, traigas, traiga, traigamos, traigáis, traigan**
venir – **venga, vengas, venga, vengamos, vengáis, vengan**

Irregularly formed are:
dar – **dé, des, dé, demos, deis, den**
estar – **esté, estés, esté, estemos, estéis, estén**
haber – **haya, hayas, haya, hayamos, hayáis, hayan**
ir – **vaya, vayas, vaya, vayamos, vayáis, vayan**
saber – **sepa, sepas, sepa, sepamos, sepáis, sepan**
ser – **sea, seas, sea, seamos, seáis, sean**

IMPERFECT SUBJUNCTIVE

This is formed from the third person plural of the preterite tense
and there are no exceptions to the rule. Each verb has two forms
– the **-ra** forms and the **-se** forms. Some examples:
tomar – **tomara, tomaras, tomara, tomáramos, tomarais,**
tomaran
tomase, tomases, tomase, tomásemos, tomaseis, tomasen
comer – **comiera, comieras, comiera, comiéramos, comierais,**
comieran
comiese, comieses, comiese, comiésemos, comieseis,
comiesen

ir/ser – fuera, fueras, fuera, fuéramos, fuerais, fueran
**   fuese, fueses, fuese, fuésemos, fueseis, fuesen**
andar – anduviera/anduviese; caer – cayera/cayese; dormir –
durmiera/durmiese; conducir – condujera/condujese; dar –
diera/diese; decir – dijera/dijese; estar – estuviera/estuviese;
haber – hubiera/hubiese; hacer – hiciera/hiciese; oír – oyera/oyese;
poder – pudiera/pudiese; poner – pusiera/pusiese; querer –
quisiera/quisiese; saber – supiera/supiese; tener – tuviera/tuviese;
traer – trajera/trajese; venir – viniera/viniese

The present subjunctive of **haber** and a past participle form
the perfect subjunctive: **haya vivido.** The imperfect subjunctive
of **haber** plus past participle form the pluperfect subjunctive:
hubiera sabido.

M   Verbs – Uses of the Subjunctive

1   To form the **usted/ustedes** imperatives and all negative
    imperatives. See Appendix C.
2   After verbs of asking, telling, persuading, wanting,
    expecting such as **pedir, decir, persuadir, querer, esperar:**
    me pidió que fuera; dígale que lo compre.
3   After verbs of emotion like **gustar, esperar** *to hope,* **sentir:**
    no me gusta que estés aquí, siento que haya venido.
4   After verbs of doubting and verbs of thinking and believing
    used negatively: **dudo que vengan; no creo que lo tenga.**
5   After certain impersonal expressions such as **más vale que,**
    importa que, no es que, no parece que, es una pena que: **no**
    le importaba que llegásemos tarde.
6   After expressions of possibility like **tal vez, probablemente:**
    tal vez ya hayan llegado.
7   After conjunctions of time like **cuando, en cuanto, antes**
    que, después que, mientras when future time is implied:
    antes que vaya; cuando estés en España; en cuanto salgan.
8   After the conjunctions **para que, con tal que, a menos**
    que, sin que, aunque (when contrary to fact):
    le di dinero para que comprase el coche; aunque fuera rico
    no lo compraría.
9   After a negative or indefinite antecedent: **busco alguien**
    que hable inglés; no hay nadie que pueda ayudarme.

10   After **que** with the sense of *may:* **que en paz descanse**
      may he rest in peace; **que duermas bien** *(may you) sleep well.*
11   In various fixed expressions like **como quieras, como usted**
      diga which are best memorized.
12   The imperfect subjunctive is always used after **como si:**
      como si tuviera mucho dinero.
13   The imperfect subjunctive is used after **si** when the
      condition is contrary to fact or unfulfilled:
      si estuviera Juan, sabría que hacer;
      si salieras temprano, podríamos coger el vuelo de las ocho.
14   The imperfect subjunctive can be used to replace the
      conditional tense; **quisiera ir; me gustara probarlo.**

N   The Articles

Definite *(the)*	**el**	(masc. sing.)	**la**	(fem. sing.)
	los	(masc. plur.)	**las**	(fem. plur.)
Indefinite *(a/an)*	**un**	(masc. sing.)	**una**	(fem. sing.)
(some)	**unos**	(masc. plur.)	**unas**	(fem. plur.)

O   Adjectives

These agree in number and gender with the noun or pronoun
they describe.
Adjectives ending in **-o** change the **o** to **a** in the feminine:
blanco – blanca. They add **-s** to form the plural: **blancos,**
blancas.
Adjectives ending in **-e** do not have a feminine form and add
-s to form the plural: **verde – verdes.**
Adjectives ending in a consonant, unless the ending is **-án** or
-or, keep the same form in the feminine and add **-es** for the
plural: **fácil – fáciles.**
Adjectives of nationality ending in a consonant add **-a** to form
the feminine: **español – española, españoles – españolas;**
inglés – inglesa, ingleses – inglesas; alemán – alemana, alemanes
– alemanas. Note the dropping of the accent in **inglés** and
alemán in the feminine and plural forms.
Adjectives ending in **-z** change the **z** to **ces** in the plural:
feliz – felices.

Position: Most adjectives follow the noun they describe: **un piso grande, unos turistas franceses.** The following usually precede the noun: **alguno, bueno, cierto, malo, medio, mucho, ninguno, otro, poco, próximo, último, varios. Grande** before a noun usually means *great –* **una gran película** *a great film;* after a noun it refers to size – **un cine grande** *a big movie theater.*

Apocopation: These adjectives drop the final **o** when they come before a noun: **alguno – algún; bueno – buen; malo – mal; ninguno – ningún; primero – primer; tercero – tercer.** This applies only to the masculine singular. **Grande** shortens to **gran** before any singular noun.

COMPARATIVE AND SUPERLATIVE

Comparative = **más** + adjective + **que**
> **Julio es más alto que Pepe** *Julio is taller than Pepe*
> **Las casas son más caras que los pisos** *The houses are more expensive than the apartments*

Superlative = **el/la/los/las** + **más** + adjective
> **Este hotel es el más lujoso de todos** *This hotel is the most luxurious of all*
> **Son los más baratos** *They're the cheapest*

There are some irregular comparatives and superlatives:
bueno *good* **mejor** *better* **el/la mejor, los/las mejores** *best*
malo *bad* **peor** *worse* **el/la peor, los/las peores** *worst*
grande *big, great* **mayor** *bigger, greater, older* **el/la mayor, los/las mayores** *biggest, greatest, oldest*
pequeño *small* **menor** *smaller, younger* **el/la menor, los/las menores** *smallest, youngest*

Normally **más grande** and **más pequeño** are used to refer to size with **mayor** and **menor** reserved for age.

P   Subject Pronouns

yo *I;* **tú** *you* (singular – friend, relative, child, pet);
él *he, it;* **ella** *she, it;* **ello** *it* (unspecific); **usted** *you* (singular – formal, acquaintances, strangers, elders); **nosotros** (masc.), **nosotras** (fem.) *we;* **vosotras** (masc.), **vosotras** (fem.) *you* (plural of **tú**); **ellos** (masc.), **ellas** (fem.) *they;* **ustedes** *you* (plural of **usted**).

Q   Object Pronouns

Direct			Indirect	
me	*me*		**me**	*to me*
te	*you*		**te**	*to you*
lo	*him, it, you* (masc.)		**le**	*to him, to her, to it, to you*
la	*her, it, you* (fem.)			
le	*you*			
nos	*us*		**nos**	*to us*
os	*you*		**os**	*to you*
los	*them, you* (masc.)		**les**	*to them, to you*
las	*them, you* (fem.)			
les	*them, you* (masc./fem.)			

These pronouns normally precede the verb: **lo veo, no me conoce, no lo hagas.**
They are added to the end of positive imperatives: **hágalo, dime.**
They are also added to infinitives and gerunds or may be placed before a verb on which the infinitive or gerund depends: **voy a tomarlo/lo voy a tomar; está mirándola/la está mirando.**
If two object pronouns come together the indirect precedes: **me lo dieron; se las enseñé.**
Le and **les** become **se** when they precede **lo, la, le, los,las** and **les.**

R   Possessives

ADJECTIVES

mi, mis *my;* **tu, tus** *your;* **su, sus** *his, her, its,your;* **nuestro/a, nuestros/as** *our;* **vuestro/a, vuestros/as** *your;* **su, sus** *their, your.*

PRONOUNS

el mío, la mía, los míos, las mías *mine*
el tuyo, la tuya, los tuyos, las tuyas *yours*
el suyo, la suya, los suyos, las suyas *his, hers, its, yours*
el nuestro, la nuestra, los nuestros, las nuestras *ours*
el vuestro, la vuestra, los vuestros, las vuestras *yours*
el suyo, la suya, los suyos, las suyas *theirs, yours*

S Cardinal Numbers

0 cero	11 once	22 veintidós	50 cincuenta
1 uno, una	12 doce	23 veintitrés	60 sesenta
2 dos	13 trece	24 veinticuatro	70 setenta
3 tres	14 catorce	25 veinticinco	80 ochenta
4 cuatro	15 quince	26 veintiséis	90 noventa
5 cinco	16 dieciséis	27 veintisiete	100 ciento
6 seis	17 diecisiete	28 veintiocho	101 ciento uno
7 siete	18 dieciocho	29 veintinueve	200 doscientos
8 ocho	19 diecinueve	30 treinta	300 trescientos
9 nueve	20 veinte	31 treinta y uno	400 cuatrocientos
10 diez	21 veintiuno	40 cuarenta	500 quinientos

600 seiscientos	700 setecientos
800 ochocientos	900 novecientos
1000 mil	1990 mil novecientos noventa
2000 dos mil	1,000,000 un millón (de)

GLOSSARY OF
GRAMMATICAL TERMS

Glossary of Grammatical Terms

Active
A verb is in the active voice if it is used to describe an action done by the subject of a sentence or phrase. Eg: He *talked* to the agent.

Adjective
An adjective is a word used to describe a noun. Eg: a *new* office.

Adverb
An adverb is a word used to modify the meaning of a verb or adjective. Eg: They *quickly* left the restaurant. It had been a *very* good meal. (Adverbs that modify adjectives as in the second example are sometimes called INTENSIFIERS.)

Article
The INDEFINITE ARTICLE is used in front of a noun which has not previously been defined by some specific reference. Eg: There's *a* lamp on that table. The indefinite article in Spanish changes according to the gender of the noun it precedes. The DEFINITE ARTICLE is placed before a noun which is already specifically established in the speaker's mind – either by prior or implied reference or by convention. Eg: We visited an exhibition; *the* exhibition was at *the* Barbican.

Clause
A component of a sentence which contains its own subject and predicate.

Comparative
The form of an adjective or adverb that enables a comparison between two things. Eg: This is *better* than that. I read it *more quickly*.

Conjunction
A word or group of words which connect nouns, phrases and clauses. *And, but, in spite of,* are all conjunctions for example.

Conjugation
The way the verb endings change according to tense and person.

Conditional
Refers to a clause that indicates what *would* happen if a certain set of circumstances prevailed. Also the tense used in such a clause.

Gender
Each noun in Spanish belongs to a gender – either MASCULINE or FEMININE.

Gerund
The part of the verb ending in *-ing* in English which is used to form continuous tenses. The Spanish equivalent ends in **-ando** or **-iendo** (sometimes **-yendo**).

Imperative
The form of a verb indicating a command.

Indicative
The indicative mood of a verb indicates an action or state which actually exists. Eg: We *are going* home. (Compare with SUBJUNCTIVE.)

Infinitive
The "to –" form of a verb, indicated in Spanish by the ending **-ar, -er** or **-ir.**

Inflection
A general term to describe the way endings of nouns, adjectives, pronouns and verbs change. Spanish is a more highly inflected language than English.

Intransitive
A verb is said to be intransitive if it does not take an object. Eg: The sun *is shining.*

Modal
Applied to verbs which indicate moods or mental attitudes. Eg: *should, can, might.*

Mood
Whether a verb is subjunctive or indicative (or imperative).

Noun
A word which names a person or thing. There are COMMON NOUNS (eg: *dog, cat, person, air*) and PROPER NOUNS (eg: *George, Mercedes, Africa*).

Number
Whether a noun, verb, adjective etc. is singular or plural.

Object
The object of a verb is the person or thing acted upon by the verb. Eg: The boxer hit the *punching bag*.

Passive
A verb is in the passive voice if it is used to describe an action done to the subject (or implied subject) of a sentence. Eg: The book *was written* by Cervantes.

Person
A term used to describe the form of a verb. The FIRST PERSON SINGULAR of a verb is the "I" form, the SECOND PERSON SINGULAR is the "you" form and so on.

Phrase
A group of words which does not constitute a grammatically complete sentence.

Plural
More than one.

Possessives
Adjectives and pronouns which indicate ownership. Eg: *my, his, mine, yours* etc.

Predicate
A word or group of words which says something about the subject. Eg: The weather *is fine today*.

Prefix
An element that precedes the main body of a noun or verb and modifies its meaning.

Preposition
A preposition is a word or group of words that establishes place, direction, method and so on. Eg: *by, with, from,* etc.

Pronoun
A word that stands for a noun or noun phrase. There are PERSONAL PRONOUNS (*I, you, me, he,* etc.), INTERROGATIVE PRONOUNS (*who, what, when, how,* etc.) and RELATIVE PRONOUNS (*where, which, that, who,* etc.)

Root (or Radical) changing verbs
Verbs in which the root vowel changes when it bears the stress of the word. The vowels affected in Spanish are **e,** which changes to **ie** or **i; o,** which changes to **ue** and sometimes **u;** and **u,** which changes to **ue.**

Sentence
A group of words that contains subject and predicate and which is a complete utterance.

Singular
Just one.

Stem
Applied to verbs and nouns to mean that portion of the word which carries meaning but not inflection (ending).

Subject
The person or thing that performs the action in a sentence. Eg: The *lion* strolled round its cage.

Subjunctive
The form of a verb that expresses a state which does not actually exist but (often) which the speaker hopes or wishes were the case. Eg: I wish that we *weren't* going.

Suffix
An element that is added to the end of a word to change its meaning.

Superlative
The form of an adjective or adverb that is employed to denote that the word it qualifies is the leader of its class. Eg: *(the) best, worst,* etc.

Tense
The form of a verb which indicates the time and duration of an action. Remember, however, that in Spanish the conventions for using tenses are not quite the same as in English – so that the present tense can often be used to refer to future actions, for example. The main tenses in Spanish are:
PRESENT, PERFECT, IMPERFECT, PRETERITE, PLUPERFECT, FUTURE, CONDITIONAL.

Transitive
A transitive verb is one which takes an object, that is, which transfers the action from the subject to another person or thing.

Verb
A word that expresses an action or state.

Voice
Whether a verb is active or passive.

ALPHABETICAL VOCABULARY

Alphabetical vocabulary

A

abajo *4.2.P1*
abierto *1.2.P5*
abogado *1.2.P4*
abrir *3.2.P2*
abrocharse *1.2.S6*
absolutamente *2.2.S1*
abundante *4.1.S2*
abundar *4.1.S1*
aburrirse *2.2.S1*
acabar de *1.1.S3*
acabarse *4.1.S6*
acceso *2.1.S2*
aceptar *1.1.S6*
acertado *2.1.S6*
aclarar *1.1.S4*
acompañar *1.1.P1*
aconsejable *3.1.S4*
aconsejar *1.2.S6*
acordar (ue) *3.1.S2*
acordar (ue) *3.2.P2*
acordarse (ue) de *2.2.S3*
estar acostumbrado *2.2.S3*
acostumbrarse *1.1.P4*
acuerdo *3.1.S5*
de acuerdo *1.1.P4*
de acuerdo con *4.1.S1*
ponerse de acuerdo *3.2.P3*
por adelantado *2.1.S1*
adelante *1.1.S5*
más adelante *3.1.P2*
además de *1.1.P7*
adjunto le remito *2.1.S6*
adquirir (ie) *1.2.S3*
afectar *1.1.S6*
afeitado *4.1.S1*

afueras *1.2.S3*
agencia de traducciones *1.1.S1*
agencia de viajes *1.2.P4*
agencia inmobiliaria *1.2.S4*
agente *1.2.S5*
agente de seguros *2.2.P2*
agradable *1.2.S4*
agradecer *1.2.S3*
quedar agradecido *2.1.S4*
agrado *4.2.S5*
agua *4.2.S5*
aguantar *4.2.P4*
ahí *1.1.S2*
ahí debajo *1.1.S4*
ahí fuera *1.1.S2*
al menos *1.1.P4*
alegrarse *1.2.S6*
alegre *1.1.S1*
alemán/alemana *1.2.P3*
Alemania *1.2.P3*
alfabético *2.1.P2*
algo *1.1.P2*
algo así como *1.1.S1*
algo de *2.1.S1*
algo es algo *4.1.S5*
algo que ver con *2.1.S6*
alguien *1.1.P2*
algún(o) *1.2.P5*
allá tú *4.1.S4*
allí *1.1.S1*
alojamiento *2.1.S3*
alquilar *2.1.P1*
alquiler *2.1.S1*
altavoz *4.2.S6*
alto *2.1.P4*
amable *2.2.S2*

ambiente *2.2.P3*
ambos *4.2.P1*
amistoso *2.1.P3*
¡por el amor de Dios! *1.1.S6*
amplio *2.1.S2, 3.1.S4*
añadir *3.1.S3*
andar *1.2.S4*
¿cómo anda de? *2.2.S2*
andarse con cuidado *3.1.S1*
año *2.1.P1*
a los tres años *2.1.P1*
anoche *1.2.S1*
de antemano *4.1.S1*
anterior *4.2.S4*
antes *1.2.S2*
antes de *1.1.S1*
lo antes posible *2.2.S2*
antojarse *3.1.S1*
anunciar *4.2.S6*
anuncio *1.1.S1*
apagar *1.2.S6. 4.2.P2*
sí, al aparato *1.1.S3*
aparcamiento *2.1.P1*
aparcar *1.1.S1*
aparecer *3.2.S3*
aparentar *2.2.S3*
apartamento de soltero *2.1.S4*
aparte *2.1.S6*
apoyar *3.1.S4*
aprender *1.1.P1*
apretar (ie) *3.1.S3*
apropiado *4.2.S4*
apuro *2.1.P4*
aquél *3.2.P1*
aquí *1.1.P2*
archivar *3.2.P2*
archivo *2.1.P2*
armar un gran lío *1.1.S4*
armario *3.2.S2*
arrancar *4.2.S6*

arreglar *1.1.P5*
arreglarse *1.2.S2*
en la parte de arriba *4.2.P1*
arriendo *2.1.S1*
ascensor *2.1.S1*
asegurarse *3.1.S5*
asesora jurídica *2.1.P5*
asesoría de empresas *1.2.S6*
así es *1.1.S2*
así por las buenas *1.1.S5*
asistente *2.2.S4*
asistir *3.1.P2*
aspecto *4.1.S2*
astucia *4.1.S1*
astuto *4.1.S1*
asunto *4.2.S1*
atender a *2.2.P5*
atentamente *1.2.P3*
aterrizar *1.2.S6*
atraer *3.1.S5*
atreverse *2.2.P3*
atrevido *1.2.S1*
aumentar *3.2.S2*
aún *1.2.S6*
aunque *1.1.P6*
avance *3.2.S4*
avance tecnológico *3.1.S2*
avanzado *3.1.S4*
averiado *1.2.P1*
averiguar *1.2.S1*
avión *1.2.S2*
en avión *1.1.S6*
avisar *1.2.S2*
aviso *3.1.S4*
ayer *4.2.S1*
ayuda *1.1.S5*
ayudar *1.2.S3*
azúcar *2.2.S2*
azul *1.2.S6*
de azul *2.2.S6*

causar buena impresión *1.1.S5*
caza *4.1.S2*
ceder *3.1.S5*
tener celos *4.1.S1*
celoso *1.2.S1*
cenar *1.2.S1*
centralizar *3.1.P2*
centro mismo *3.2.P3*
cerca *2.1.P1*
cerrado *3.1.S1*
cerrar (ie) *1.1.S6*
cerrarse (ie) *4.1.P1*
certificado *2.2.P2*
cierre *4.1.S1*
cierto *3.1.S3, 3.2.P1*
por cierto *4.2.S4*
cifra *4.1.S1*
cigarrillo *1.2.S6*
cine *4.2.P4*
cínico *3.1.S1*
cinturón de seguridad *1.2.S6*
ciudad *1.2.S6*
con claridad *3.2.S3*
claro *1.1.P2, 2.1.P1*
claro está *3.2.S2*
claro que *3.1.S1*
clase *1.2.S5*
clasificar *3.2.P2*
cocina *2.1.P1*
cocinar *4.1.S2*
cocinita *2.1.S1*
cóctel *2.2.P3*
coger *1.2.P4*
colchón *4.2.S5*
colega *2.2.S3*
colegio *1.2.S3*
para colmo *3.1.S5*
colonia *4.1.S1*
de color crema *1.2.S2*
comenzar (ie) *2.1.P5*

comer *1.2.P4*
cometido *4.1.S5*
comida *4.1.S2, 4.2.P5*
comité de empresas *2.2.S1*
comité de enlace *3.1.S2*
¿cómo? *1.1.P2*
como de costumbre *1.1.S2*
¿cómo es? *4.1.S2*
¿cómo que no? *1.1.S6*
como quiera *1.2.P5*
como siempre *2.1.P3*
¿cómo te va? *2.1.P3*
como usted diga *4.2.S2*
cómodo *1.2.S3*
compañero *4.2.P2*
compañía *1.1.P7*
compartir *4.1.S6*
competencia *2.1.S6*
complacer *2.1.S6*
complicar *4.2.S3*
componer *4.2.P1*
comportarse *2.1.S5*
comprar *1.2.S2*
comprender *1.1.P1, 3.2.S4*
comprobar *2.2.P1*
con que sí *4.1.S1*
conceder *4.1.S1*
concluir *4.2.P1*
concurrir *4.1.P1*
concursar *4.1.P1*
concurso *4.1.S1*
conducir *3.1.P3, 4.1.S6*
conductor *3.1.P3*
conectar *4.1.S6, 4.2.P2*
confirmar *2.2.S5*
conmigo *2.2.S1*
no lo voy a conocer *3.1.S5*
conocerse *1.1.P6, 3.2.S3*
conocido *4.1.P4*
conociendo *3.2.S2*

más bien *1.2.S2*
más de *3.2.S6*
no ... más que *1.1.S6*
material rodante *3.2.S4*
mayor *2.1.S2*
mayoría *4.1.S1*
mayúscula *2.2.P4*
mecánico *1.2.P1*
mecanógrafa *2.2.S2*
mecanografía *2.2.S2*
media hora *1.2.P4*
medianoche *2.2.S5*
medicina *4.2.P5*
médico *4.2.S5*
medios *3.2.S6*
medir (i) *2.1.S1*
mejor ordenada *1.1.P5*
lo mejor *4.2.S4*
a lo mejor *1.2.S1*
mejorar *3.2.S6*
menos mal *1.2.S2*
mensaje *1.2.P1*
mensual *3.1.S2*
merecer *3.1.S1*
merecer la pena *2.2.S4*
merendar (ie) *2.2.S6*
merluza *4.1.S2*
mes pasado *1.2.S2*
mes que viene *3.2.S5*
mesa *3.2.S2*
mesita *1.1.P5*
meter *1.1.S5*
meterse *3.1.S6, 4.1.S4*
metro cuadrado *2.1.S1*
mezclar *3.1.S4*
a mí también *1.1.P6*
la mía *1.1.P3*
mientras que *1.2.P3*
mientras tanto *1.2.P2*
miércoles *1.2.P2*

millón de *1.2.S6*
mínimo *3.1.P4*
misión *3.1.P2*
mismo *1.2.S3, 2.1.P5*
aquel mismo día *1.1.P5*
con moderación *4.2.P5*
modo *4.1.S1*
de ese modo *1.1.P1*
de modo distinto *1.1.P5*
de todos modos *1.2.S4, 4.2.S4*
de momento *1.2.S3*
moneda *3.1.P1*
montar *1.2.S6*
moreno *2.1.S5*
mostrar (ue) *3.2.S2*
mostrarse (ue) *3.1.S2, 4.2.S3*
motor *3.2.S4*
mover (ue) *1.1.P5*
mujer *1.1.P1*
multicopista *4.2.P2*
mundo *1.1.P7*
todo el mundo *4.1.S1*
municipio *3.1.S2*
música *2.2.P3*

N
nacionalidad *1.2.P3*
nada *1.1.S6*
nada de nuevo *2.2.S6*
nada que hacer *3.1.S6*
nadie *1.1.S2*
nadie más *4.2.S2*
naranja *2.2.P3*
sin necesidad *4.2.S3*
necesario *3.2.S2*
negocios *1.1.P7*
negociaciones *4.1.P4*
ni yo tampoco *1.2.S1*
ninguno *2.1.S1*
nivel *2.1.S6*

subir a pie *2.1.S1*
sucio *4.1.S1*
sucursal *1.1.P7*
sueco *4.1.S1*
sueldo *2.1.S5*
suerte *2.1.S5*
tener suerte *2.2.S3*
suficiente *1.2.P5*
sugerir (ie) *4.2.P5*
sumo *3.1.S2*
superior *4.2.P2*
suponer que sí *1.1.S2*
era de suponer *4.1.S1*
es de suponer *4.1.P5*
eso ya me lo suponía *1.2.S4*
sur *2.1.S1*
suspender *3.2.S1*
sustituir *1.1.S3*
no es lo suyo *4.2.S4*

T
tabique *2.1.S1*
tal *3.2.P2*
tal cosa *3.1.S5*
tal vez *1.1.S4*
¿qué tal? *1.2.S3*
¿qué tal te fue? *3.1.S5*
taller de máquinas *3.2.S4*
tamaño *2.1.S1*
tampoco *1.1.P5*
tan *1.1.S1*
tanto *1.1.P4*
tantos *3.2.P2*
tapa *4.2.P2*
taquigrafía *2.2.S2*
tardar en *1.2.P5*
tarde *1.1.S2*
de la tarde *1.2.P5*
por la tarde *1.1.P5*
tarjeta de crédito *1.2.S5*

tarjeta de embarque *1.2.S6*
tarjeta de identificación *2.2.S6*
tarjeta postal *1.2.S1*
taza *1.1.P6*
técnico diseñador *3.1.S2*
tecnología *3.1.S2*
tema *1.1.P4*
temerse que no *2.1.P4*
temerse que sí *1.2.S2*
temporada *4.1.S2*
tendido de vías *3.2.S4*
tener *1.1.S2*
allí tiene *1.1.S1*
¿qué tiene de malo? *4.1.S3*
¿qué tiene usted? *4.2.P5*
tener éxito *2.1.S5*
tener que *1.1.S2*
tiene que haber *1.1.S6*
tenga *1.2.S5, 2.2.S5*
terminar *2.1.S5*
terreno *1.2.S4, 3.2.S4*
hace un tiempo ideal *2.1.S5*
tanto tiempo *4.1.P4*
tengo poco tiempo *1.1.P2*
tienda *2.1.P1*
tilde *2.2.P4*
tinto *3.1.P1*
tío *3.1.S5*
tipo *3.1.P4*
tirar *4.2.S5*
tirar de *4.2.P2*
título *2.2.P2*
todas estas cosas *1.1.S2*
todo *1.1.S2*
todos *1.1.S1*
tomate *4.1.P2*
tónica con ginebra *3.1.P1*
tonterías *3.2.S1*
hacer el tonto *4.2.S4*
tortilla *3.1.P1*

otra vez *1.2.S1*
otra vez será *3.1.S5*
una y otra vez *1.1.P1*
viabilidad *3.2.S5*
viajar *3.2.P5*
viaje *1.2.S1*
de viaje *3.2.P5*
viaje de negocios *3.1.P5*
vida *3.2.S4*
viejo *1.1.P4*
viernes *1.2.P2*
vivir *1.2.P3*
volante *3.1.P3*
volver (ue) *1.1.S4, 1.2.P4*
volver (ue) a *1.2.S1*
volver (ue) loco *2.2.P3*
voy tirando *2.1.P3*
vuelo *1.2.S3*
vuelo de vuelta *1.2.S5*

vuelta *4.1.P2*
dar una vuelta *3.2.S2*
de vuelta *2.2.P1*
estar de vuelta *2.1.S3*

W
wáter *2.1.S1*

Y
¿y qué? *4.1.S4*
ya *1.1.P6*
ya está *4.2.S1*
ya no lo es *1.1.S4*
ya no *1.1.S3*

Z
zona *2.1.S1*
zumo *3.2.S1*

LANGUAGE AND REFERENCE BOOKS

Dictionaries and References
VOX Spanish and English Dictionaries
Cervantes-Walls Spanish and English Dictionary
Klett German and English Dictionary
NTC's New College French & English Dictionary
NTC's New College Greek & English Dictionary
Zanichelli New College Italian & English Dictionary
Zanichelli Super-Mini Italian & English Dictionary
NTC's Dictionary of Spanish False Cognates
NTC's Dictionary of German False Cognates
NTC's Dictionary of *Faux Amis*
NTC's American Idioms Dictionary
NTC's Dictionary of American Slang and
  Colloquial Expressions
Forbidden American English
Essential American Idioms
Contemporary American Slang
Everyday American English Dictionary
Everyday American Phrases in Content
Beginner's Dictionary of American English Usage
NTC's Dictionary of Grammar Terminology
Robin Hyman's Dictionary of Quotations
Guide to Better English Spelling
303 Dumb Spelling Mistakes
NTC's Dictionary of Literary Terms
The Writer's Handbook
Diccionario Inglés
El Diccionario Básico Norteamericano
British/American Language Dictionary
The French-Speaking World
The Spanish-Speaking World
Guide to Spanish Idioms
Guide to German Idioms
Guide to French Idioms
101 Japanese Idioms
Au courant
Guide to Correspondence in Spanish
Guide to Correspondence in French
Español para los Hispanos
Business Russian
Yes! You Can Learn a Foreign Language
Japanese in Plain English
Korean in Plain English
Easy Chinese Phrasebook and Dictionary
Japan Today!
Everything Japanese
Easy Hiragana
Easy Katakana
Easy Kana Workbook
The Wiedza Powszechna Compact Polish & English
  Dictionary

Picture Dictionaries
English; French; Spanish; German

Let's Learn...Picture Dictionaries
English, Spanish, French, German, Italian

Verb References
Complete Handbook of Spanish Verbs
Complete Handbook of Russian Verbs
Spanish Verb Drills
French Verb Drills
German Verb Drills

Grammar References
Spanish Verbs and Essentials of Grammar
Nice 'n Easy Spanish Grammar
French Verbs and Essentials of Grammar
Real French
Nice 'n Easy French Grammar
German Verbs and Essentials of Grammar
Nice 'n Easy German Grammar
Italian Verbs and Essentials of Grammar
Essentials of Russian Grammar
Essentials of English Grammar
Roots of the Russian Language
Reading and Translating Contemporary Russian
Essentials of Latin Grammar
Swedish Verbs and Essentials of Grammar

Welcome to...Books
Spain, France, Ancient Greece, Ancient Rome

Language Programs: Audio and Video
Just Listen 'n Learn: Spanish, French, Italian, German,
  Greek
Just Listen 'n Learn PLUS: Spanish, French, German
Speak French
Speak Spanish
Speak German
Practice & Improve Your...Spanish, French, Italian,
  German
Practice & Improve Your...Spanish PLUS, French PLUS,
  Italian PLUS, German PLUS
Improve Your...Spanish, French, Italian, German: The
  P & I Method
Conversational...in 7 Days: Spanish, French, German,
  Italian, Portuguese, Greek, Russian, Japanese, Thai
Everyday Japanese
Japanese for Children
Nissan's Business Japanese
Contemporary Business Japanese
Basic French Conversation
Basic Spanish Conversation
Everyday Hebrew
VideoPassport in French and Spanish
How to Pronounce Russian Correctly
How to Pronounce Spanish Correctly
How to Pronounce French Correctly
How to Pronounce Italian Correctly
How to Pronounce Japanese Correctly
L'Express: Ainsi va la France
L'Express: Aujourd'hui la France
Der Spiegel: Aktuelle Themen in der Bundesrepublik
  Deutschland
Listen and Say It Right in English
Once Upon a Time in Spanish, French, German
Let's Sing & Learn in French & Spanish

"Just Enough" Phrase Books
Chinese, Dutch, French, German, Greek, Hebrew,
  Hungarian, Italian, Japanese, Portuguese, Russian,
  Scandinavian, Serbo-Croat, Spanish
Business French, Business German, Business Spanish

Language Game and Humor Books
Easy French Vocabulary Games
Easy French Crossword Puzzles
Easy French Word Games and Puzzles
Easy French Grammar Puzzles
Easy Spanish Word Power Games
Easy Spanish Crossword Puzzles
Easy Spanish Vocabulary Puzzles
Easy French Word Games and Puzzles
Easy French Culture Games
Easy German Crossword Puzzles
Easy Italian Crossword Puzzles
Let's Learn about Series: Italy, France, Germany, Spain,
  America
Let's Learn Coloring Books in Spanish, French, German,
  Italian, English
Let's Learn...Spanish, French, German, Italian, English
  Coloring Book-Audiocassette Package
My World in...Coloring Books: Spanish, French,
  German, Italian
German à la Cartoon
Spanish à la Cartoon
French à la Cartoon
101 American English Idioms
El alfabeto
L'alphabet

Getting Started Books
Introductory language books in Spanish, French,
  German, Italian

Ticket to...Series
France, Germany, Spain, Italy (Guide and audiocassette)

Getting to Know...Series
France, Germany, Spain, Italy,
  Mexico, United States

PASSPORT BOOKS
a division of *NTC Publishing Group*
Lincolnwood, Illinois USA